Legal Mail Window

The Autobiography by
Bernard "Tribe" Ackon

Legal Mail Window LLC

ISBN: 979-8-9955945-8-1

Library of Congress Control Number: Pending

Title: Legal Mail Window

Author: Bernard Ackon

Paperback Edition | 2024

"Till remaining the same hurts more than change, you will remain the same."

-Kenneth Durham (D-dorm bunk #321)

Table of Contents

Prologue

Donnie Gibson was walking through the halls. Just another day in Marion Correctional Facility, in Ocala FL. He goes to see an acquaintance, Sal, in A3 to buy 2 packs of rips, which is another word for cigarettes in the chain gang. Donnie proceeded through the halls making small talk with random people. Someone yells from across the hall "hey Donnie 16 more years and a wake up!" Just trying to be funny, as Donnie snickers at his comment. Donnie knows he's not going anywhere. He is serving 50 years for accessory to murder. The irony of it was that he was just a passenger in a vehicle. Donnie and a bunch of his friends were at his home on the porch when a car pulled up and told him to hop in the car. Donnie was a gang member and according to gang rules when someone pulls up like that and tells you to "ride" you don't ask questions. They rode together and pulled up on a few rival members and shot four of them injuring two, critically, and killing the other two. Donnie was in the back seat on the passenger side and had no weapon, but gangs have a "no-snitching" policy and just had to accept the time he got. Since then, Donnie has been filing motions for the past 13 years in which all of them have been denied. He had one motion left floating in the system which was filed five years ago. Donnie sat at his bunk to roll up his rips when he was approached by the ticket man. The ticket man is who the streets call a "bookie" and hands out tickets in which you select your winning teams for the games coming up that evening. Donnie takes his tickets and begins to select his teams when a call comes on the intercom. "The following inmates report to legal mail window after chow....". 12 names were called including Donnie's name. He froze. At this point even he forgot he still had a motion still pending. A shockwave flowed through his body. He put his cigs down and said a prayer. "Lord I cannot do this anymore. You see my situation. I haven't been the best man, yet I am still your child. I have been here for nearly 20 years. Make a way, please." Chow time everyone lined up and proceeded to get their trays in a single file line. Donnie got his and sat down but didn't touch anything on the tray. His nerves were shot. The anticipation of what was going to happen or what wasn't going to happen ruined any appetite he had. The other three inmates at his table asked if he was going to eat and Donnie told them no, they could have it. They all scrambled to grab what they wanted off the tray, then Donnie knocked on the table and got up and proceeded to throw the empty tray into the disposal. As Donnie approached the legal mail window you could see about 15 other people standing there as the rain continued to pour down heavily. No overhead covering to block the rain and some of the inmates have important papers to mail out which they had wrapped up in black trash bags, so the paperwork does not get wet. The line was very quiet. Everyone had their own stress, and fight, praying something comes through that window for them. Donnie's turn came up in line as the rain continued to batter his state issue cap. Donnie showed his ID and was handed a brown manila envelope packet which he tucked into his shirt as he made his way back to the dorm. Donnie arrived back at the dorm and proceeded to open that envelope in a nervous wreck. The first paper out of the packet was an intro telling him that his motion had been denied and that his judgment had been affirmed. Donnie smiled and sat in a stoic state as if the universe had tried his whole being and expected a reaction from him. The TV was on in the day room and everyone in the dorms was done with chow and was changing into their shorts and white T-shirts to go to the yard for recreation (rec). One of the inmates passed by Donnie's cell and found him hanging with the sheet from the bed tied to the bunk. The inmate immediately alerted the correctional officers as they ran to the cell yelling "code red!" Next to his lifeless body lay the first page, as if it had floated to the ground while the rest of the packet was still on the bed. He never read the rest. That first page was all he needed to know.

1

August 16th 2007

I woke up from a nightmare. I dreamt that I was being attacked by demons. I saw my girlfriend in the dream with all these punk rock clothes on and piercings all over. What was odd was that it was not even her style. In the dream, we were not together, even though we had been together for 10 years up to that point. There were no signs or indications of a break up, but for some reason, I just knew. I woke up from the dream that morning and called her. She was at work doing hair when I called, per usual, and she sounded calm as I began telling her the dream I had. She then told me how weird it was and that she would never leave me and not think like that. She also said do not worry about it is just a dream.

I then hung up the phone. I was assured because 10 years was a long time for my 27-year-old self. We have two kids, six and eight years old. I began looking for my cigarettes, but I could not find them. After about two minutes of looking, I heard, "Search warrant!

Search warrant!" and banging on the front door.

I frantically ran to the garage. My dog Jade thinks I am playing currently, so she chases me and I almost trip. I finally made it to the garage.

We were renting, and the house was already furnished when we moved in, and the garage consisted of doors and door products. It was as if the owner used to make doors there because it had a workbench and doorknobs and locks everywhere. I quickly turn off the light and hide under the workbench. My dog kept licking me, so I was whispering and yelling telling her to stop.

I hear people in the house, and I am hoping they don't come to the garage.

In the house there is a middle section, there is a corridor that separates the hallway from the garage and that is where the washer and dryer are. No one came into the garage because of the dog barking ferociously, which gave me time to figure out my next Move. One of the police officers attempted to come through the garage but my dog lunged at the female officer, and she tried to scramble out of there in the process hitting her shin against the washing machine.

About an hour went by and I figured every officer was inside the house. I was just ready to make a run for it. I was listening to hear outside and did not hear anyone outside. So, with my hands on the garage door, I counted to three then raised the garage quickly and made a run for it. To my surprise, three officers were already standing outside telling me to get on the ground, and at the same time my dog (once again thinking we were playing) clipped me and I fell. The officers pointed AK-47 assault rifles at me as I lay prostrate on the ground. I do not blame my dog one bit because she was so loyal and protective that she formed a barrier around me to where the officers could not touch me, and they were about to shoot her. I yelled for them not to shoot my dog. "I can get her under control. Please let me get up and get the dog." After a bit of commotion, eventually, they agreed, and with one command along with a finger snap, my dog calmed down and followed me back into the house. Sergeant Brieske was the first to question me and asked if I knew what I was being arrested for. I told him I had no idea. He told me Sale and Delivery of cocaine and possession of Cocaine. I then asked him how it was possible when I did not have anything in the house. Then he told me it was from a previous sale. I asked for a lawyer immediately then he said these exact words,

"Get comfortable you're going to be in Jail for a long time."

Now I have been arrested numerous times by this particular officer turned sergeant and he always said this same quote to me. Here is a quick backstory on that.

In 1999, I used to sell pot to make ends meet. There was a man by the name of Walt that gave me a job cutting grass and at times I would get weed for him.

Walt winds up getting in trouble and sets me up to get out of his jam. One particular night I met up with him to pick up the money to get him weed in from the next town over, Fort Pierce Florida. Walt did not realize that I was there just to pick up the money and I had not gotten the weed yet. So, when I pulled up to the warehouse to meet him, he threw a hand signal up, and out of nowhere a fleet of agents came out and threw me on the ground. One officer kicked me in the chest, assuming he did that for a more dramatic effect.

They searched the scene as I was in handcuffs and they found no drugs, but they found a .45 caliber pistol in the vehicle that I was driving. Because they found no drugs but found a gun they charged me with Robbery with a Firearm. That same detective Brieske said to get comfortable, you are going to be there for a while. At that time, I was 19 so I was scared. First major case ever. I have been all through juvenile detention centers and various programs but never adult Facilities.

The plea deal went from 52 months (about 4 and a Half years) in prison to one year in the county jail with no probation. At this time, I am sitting in the back room in court in front of a piece of paper with the plea deal on it and the specially appointed lawyer (because Walt had a public defender which made it a conflict of interest) is over my back demanding I sign it.

At this time, I was 19 years old, and I had never been in a situation like this, so I did not know what to do. All the lawyer kept doing was demanding I sign the paper.

"Just sign the paper! Sign the deal!" he kept yelling. "You see they went from 52 months in prison to a year in the county jail with no probation you better sign it. When I come back in the room you better have it signed!"

I ended up signing it. Halfway through my one-year bid in the county jail that same lawyer comes to the jail to do his usual visit to his clients in jail. He calls for me and tells me, "Sorry I didn't notify you, but they had dropped the gun charge in your case." Then they sent me back to my dorm. I asked him before I left if that meant that without a gun there was no case to begin with and I am not even supposed to be doing this time in jail. He says, "That is correct however it is too late." I was furious. So, my charge is Attempted Robbery with a Deadly Weapon. This charge does not even make sense. This charge has been such a burden throughout my life. It had prevented me from getting jobs and a slew of other opportunities.

This is my only felony, and therefore I cannot have any weapons. One other time as a juvenile I ran from then detective Brieske, and he gave chase. I hit a corner and hid in the bushes, and he ran past me. I stayed in the bushes for over an hour and then a canine popped up licking my face. I was caught. Detective Brieske was for some reason so mad that I fooled him. It was at that moment he was determined to put me away. I guess I made him look foolish before his peers.

That same year detective Brieske pulled me and my pregnant girlfriend over a fictitious warrant and she wound up going into labor. She was flown to St. Mary's Hospital in West Palm

Beach while I went to the detention Center in Fort Pierce. She wound up having the baby prematurely at 26 weeks (about 6 months). My son was born weighing 1 pound and 15 ounces. Come to find out the warrant was bogus, and they let me go that same night. Fast forward to this moment.

After intensely searching the house for over three hours, all the officers found was a little bit of weed and rolling papers and a scale. They also found a safe that I had sitting in my closet that I never had a key for. The officers asked what was in the safe. I told them that nothing was in it. They grinned as they grabbed the batting ram used for the door to break the safe. Nothing. I remember seeing the frustration on their faces. They eventually told me what I was being charged with:

1. Possession of cocaine

2. Sale and delivery of cocaine

3. Possession of marijuana under 20 grams

4. Possession of paraphernalia

5. Assault on a Law Enforcement Officer

6. Possession of ammunition by a convicted felon

I asked why I was being charged with Assault on a Law enforcement officer and they said that the dog bit the police officer. My dog did not bite the police officer. They told me to tell it to the judge. My dog was taken to the pound at the same time I was going to jail. It even cost a fee to get him out which was similar to a bond. Safe to say me and my dog caught a case together.

I sat in jail that night and the next day went to the bond hearing. At the bond hearing, I had a chance to look at all the charges and read the arrest with more clarity and figure out what was going on. I was appointed a public defender for the moment, and she explained that the sale delivery and possession charges came from a previous sale that was supposedly made. They just came to serve the warrant for it. She also explained that the assault on a law enforcement officer was from your dog biting the police officer.

I immediately interjected and told her my dog did not bite anyone.

She lunged at the officer that tried to enter the garage and she fell. Secondly, even if the dog did, how can you charge me for it? She goes on to say "Well, they did, and they also found a box of ammunition, so they charged you with possession of ammunition by a convicted felon". I did not have any ammunition. I was in such confusion. The public defender goes on to say that this was a bond hearing, so they are going to state your charges and it is up to the judge to give you a bond for each of the six charges.

My turn came and we approached the judge and decided on bonds for each one:

· Sale and delivery of Cocaine $75k

· Possession of cocaine $25k

· Battery on a law enforcement officer $2.5k

· Possession of cannabis under 20 grams $500

· Possession of Paraphernalia $500

Then the judge stopped and asked about the charge of possession of ammunition and said that he had never heard of a charge like that. First, he said $10k then he said it was a dumb charge, so I am going to release him on his own recognizance (ROR) on that particular charge. That means I do not have to pay a bond for that charge and if I only had that charge, I could walk out of jail. But the total of my bond came out to $103.5k. I did not have 10% of that and collateral (which is a requirement for that high of a bond) and nobody was going to give it to me. So, I will just sit back and wait a few weeks till the next bond hearing.

A few weeks went by, and I finally got a bond reduction. The Judge reduced the bond down to around $50k which made it somewhat affordable. I was in constant contact with family members and friends. Some felt bad and were giving my girlfriend money here and there towards my bond. However, a few days later the collect calls had stopped being accepted. Nothing was going through. I began to see people that I knew coming in and eventually bonding out telling me of parties that they were being invited to at my house. I still did not fully believe it, all I knew was to tell them to tell my girlfriend to put minutes on the phone and get my bond money together. They all said they would tell her, but no one did. My best friend's name is Clutch, solid brother, who always took my calls and even sent me money when I needed it, and even he could not get a hold of her.

One day on September 7, 2007, I was on the phone with him and surprisingly my girlfriend walked by Clutch on the street. It was perfect because there was no escape now, she must take this phone call. Finally answers to all my questions. He tells her that Tribe was on the phone. She them takes the phone and says, "What Tribe?" That right there told me something was wrong. I then I asked her what was going on with the bond money my friends gave her for me and what was taking her so long to get me? she takes a deep breath and says,

"Tribe, you are not coming home. My life is better without you, and I do not need you anymore."

I just sat. Funny how silence was for a moment but the whole life I made with her flash before my eyes. This was not my first case. She has been there through previous cases and everything I had ever been through since I was 17, I am 27 currently and we have a six-year-old girl Taraina, and an eight-year-old boy named David.

My whole environment knows it is us two versus the world. My mother knows the closeness of our relationship and knows whatever Jam I was in my girlfriend was always there. So, to hear those words my heart sank. I then asked how she expected me to fight the case from here. I am facing 42 years. How would I get a lawyer? she said, "Tough figure it out."

I broke down on that phone. Two people came and carried me away to my bunk. My family would call her from time to time to find out how I was doing, and she would tell them I was ok, and that she was helping me, and my family would believe her. They did not know I was alone in this situation and when I tried to explain that she was not helping, they just thought I was delirious. So now what do I do, when I am facing all this time and no one on the outside to help me? What about my kids? They were too young to even understand. I did not eat for days as I sat in the dorm contemplating suicide. The week before that I had just lost my uncle Kofi who was very dear to me. I took the news and held it in. You know it is really bad when you begin to look at the railings on the steps when you are standing on the top tier saying to yourself, "Well if I angle the jump this way, I could hit the handles of the rail with my head and it will be less painful, or if I jump this way I can

hit the table with my neck but the tables are small so I could miss."

This was the way my mind was thinking but I could never push myself to do it. All this stress inside of a four cornered box.

2
Adapting to my environment

Been a few days already in Rock Road Jail in St. Lucie County, Florida. Been here so many times up to this point but it never gets easier. I traded Tuesday's breakfast tray for Friday's chicken tray because I couldn't stand the cornbread and slop in the morning. They don't feed you properly in here. I needed an outlet to relieve stress, so I chose to do push-ups. I usually use two plastic chairs to keep each arm on, while my legs are propped up on the table to do them. There was a person in my dorm by the name of Raheem, Haitian guy, big in size, and had a lot of family in jail and in the streets. He always had big bags of canteen, so he never needed for anything. I do not know why, but for some reason he did not like me. So, he saw me working out and the phone was in the middle of where I was working out at. Raheem approached and snatched one of the chairs from under me then picked up the phone and began calling someone. I saw how he had a lot of friends in the dorm. I knew I would've gotten jumped had I reacted, so I kept my cool for another time.

A few days later, I was writing a letter then he comes up and disrupts me. So, I get up and square up with him and we go in circles. I realized that he did not want to swing and honestly neither did I, so we walked away from each other. He went and assembled his boys and had a meeting in one of the cells in Delta East (Dorm 9). I counted 15 of them. I see them upstairs, but I pay it no attention. I am reading a newspaper in the dayroom at this time. Moments later he came downstairs and walked past me and said, "Get there!" And walked into one of the downstairs cells. I ignored him and continued reading till he got by the cell and yelled, "Tribe!!"

I was fully committed then. I proceeded to cell "C", following him in and his friend "Poobie" closed the door behind us. When those cell doors close, one will have to ring the intercom to the tower to have them open the cell doors back. The problem was inmates rang the intercom just for stupid reasons and questions. Thus began a rule that if you ring the buzzer you go to confinement (the box), automatically. As I was fighting with Raheem I noticed from the corner of my eye one person sleeping in his bed had just woken up to watch the fight, and another guy named Travis was in the corner drawing.

I got up against the wall because since Raheem was big, maybe I could tire him out by making him hit his hands against the wall with every punch thrown. It worked because as we were exchanging blows he began to slow up on the punches. I can see everyone outside pushing each other just to look through a skinny rectangular glass to watch the fight. Eventually, we both got tired and sat down, still locked in the room. There were no cameras, so the correctional officers (COs) saw nothing. I proceeded to the intercom to push the button.

The CO answers, "You guys are locked in till chow time since you guys want a horse around!" Chow time was about an hour away. We usually can tell the time by whatever show is on the television at the moment. I then said that we were not playing and the door had slammed shut by accident. All the people jumping up and down outside the door made it look like people were playing, I assumed. Then out of nowhere Travis, the other guy who was drawing, stood up and asked if he could get the "friendly," meaning we fight and be cool afterwards.

For a quick second, I remembered why he had a gripe with me. A few weeks back, we were in line to get our trays. Travis got his tray then I got mine and walked upstairs. As I was walking upstairs, Travis yelled to me, "Let me get the cookies off your tray!" We never even spoke to each other before that. I assumed he was trying to make me look like I was a punk, but I have been to jail so many times before this I know how you get treated for not sticking up for yourself. No one would help someone if they were not willing to defend themselves, it was an unwritten rule. I always feared backing down from a fight because doing that would make your living arrangement extremely uncomfortable. I jumped down the stairs so fast my tray dropped and charged at him. People stopped me in my tracks and broke it up then nothing more became of that. But I always had my eye on him. Now that he has friends in a locked room with me, he has built confidence.

Getting back to the situation, I stood up. Travis charged at me with his head down throwing his arms in complete disorder making it easy for me to directly hit him in the face. The combination of the punches to the nose made it pour blood. Travis began yelling in pain and he ran to the metal toilet. I walked up to the intercom and pressed the button again, but they ignored me. I just sat down. A few minutes later the person who was laying on top of the bunk

jumped up and asked for the "friendly."

I immediately yelled in my most intimidating voice, "Better stay up there if you know what's best for you!" I was nervous, but I could not show it. Assuming I had shown the slightest hint of scare, they all would have teamed up on me. And I probably wouldn't have come out of the cell alive. In fact, the guy on the top bunk was Raheem's cousin! He was much shorter also, so I knew Raheem was not there just to sit and watch me get the best of him.

30 minutes or so had gone by the room was so quiet and you can cut the tension with a knife. Raheem was still sitting flexing his hand from punching the wall so many times and not saying anything. His cousin was now fully awake sitting up on his bunk and Travis was still padding his wounded nose over the metal toilet. You can see the john filled with red tissue.

To everyone in that cell's surprise, Travis decided to get up and throw his hands up saying "come on and run the fight back". I asked him humbly if it could wait till after chow because there was blood all over him. He says, "Forget that come on!" So, I got back up. Unsurprisingly, Travis did the same thing again, head down and swinging his arms all over the place. I connected with his face perfectly, it seemed like it was in the same spot. Now blood poured out of his nose and this time there was a cut at the bridge where his cartilage and bone connected, and blood was squirting outward. He yelled in excruciating pain, falling to his knees. I immediately walked back to the intercom and pressed the button at least 20 times then the CO finally responded and said everyone was going to confinement after chow. I said "fine take me now". They still waited another 30 minutes or so as we all sat and waited.

That pressure was different. Then finally, the CO walks up holding four styrofoam trays stacked on top of one another and pops open the door. The look on the officer's face said it all. Blood was all over the walls and floors and the place was a mess. The CEO signaled to everyone to "roll in" and called for backup and took us all to the box. I immediately just began praising God in my mind for coming out with my life.

3

Trying to make it make sense

In confinement, I met a guy named "Revo Theory", a great, down-to-earth man and naturally talented with music. He wrote raps, sang and wrote poetry. He was from Fort Myers, Florida. Listening to his catalog made the time fly. But when he was not rapping or talking to me, I would pick up the only book I had in there, the Bible. It was a suitable place for me to read it with no distractions. I started by reading the book Psalms. I felt the Psalms because they showed me God's promises to help me and how he looks deep into the hearts and minds and protects his people. Then it got deeper to where it kept telling me to wait on God and how even my mother and father would leave me before God did.

Then I came across a scripture that I constantly kept coming back to. It was Isaiah 41:10 "Fear not for I am with you. Be not dismayed for I am your God. I will help you. I will strengthen you. I will uphold you with my victorious right hand." I held that scripture close.

One night I was laying in my bunk and decided to read, and I came across a story in the book of Genesis about a boy named Joseph who had 11 brothers. The brothers hated Joseph because he was his dad's favorite child. His dad bought him a rainbow robe which made his brothers even more jealous of him. Also, Joseph used to have weird dreams.

One particular dream was the sun, moon, and stars bowing down to him. It made his brothers hate him more, but his dad thought about it and tried to understand it. Soon after, Joseph's brothers went out to pasture their flocks. They were gone a while, so their dad sent Joseph to see what they were up to. So, Joseph put on his robe and went to see them. Now Joseph's brothers saw him coming and made plans to kill him. One of the brothers said no let us just throw him in this pit right here so he would die without us touching him. Joseph finally arrived and they pulled off his robe and threw him in the pit.

Then they saw some traders on camels passing by and figured they could just sell him at least. So they sold him and splashed the robe with goat blood and took it back to their dad. Joseph's dad was crushed thinking he was eaten by a wild animal. Meanwhile, the traders sold Joseph to an officer of Pharaoh, the king of Egypt, named Potiphar, and he was the captain of the palace guards. Now the Lord was with Joseph and blessed him greatly even while he served in the home of his Egyptian master. Joseph was successful in everything he did, and Potiphar did not want for anything, Joseph knew what Potiphar wanted before Potiphar himself even knew! Potiphar did not have a worry the world but to eat and sleep.

Now Joseph was a very handsome and well-built young man and Potiphar's wife began to desire him.

She asked Joseph numerous times to sleep with her, but Joseph always said no and that his master trusted him with everything and that he would never do such a wicked thing. After consistent pressure, Joseph was doing work inside the house and the wife figured this was her chance, so she grabbed him, and he ran off ripping off his shirt. At this time, Potiphar was in another country and entrusted Joseph with everything except his wife.

The wife called the guards and asked, "Why did her husband bring in a Hebrew slave to mock us? Look he tried to rape me, but I screamed then he ran, and I have his shirt to prove it."

Once Potiphar got wind of what happened he had Joseph put in prison. But the Lord was with Joseph even in prison! Joseph was in favor of all the guards and eventually running the prison. Sometime later pharaoh's cupbearer and Chief Baker offended the pharaoh and were put in prison.

One night the cupbearer and the chief baker had a dream and each one had its meaning. The next morning, they both had a dejected look on their face so Joseph asked them why they were upset, and they both said they had dreams they could not make out. Joseph then tells them it is God's business to interpret dreams and to tell him what they saw. The cupbearer said he saw a vine in front of him and it had three branches that began to blossom, and on them were clusters of grapes.

He was holding Pharaoh's wine cup in his hand, and he took the grapes and squeezed the juice into it. Then place the cup back into the pharaoh's hand. Joseph said the three branches meant in three days the cup bearer will be back to his position as pharaoh's cupbearer, Joseph also mentioned, ",When you do, please ask Pharaoh to let me out of here, I was kidnapped from my homeland, home of the Hebrews and did nothing wrong". Now, the Chief Baker told his dream to Joseph. He said in his dream that with three baskets of pastries on his head and in the top baskets were all kinds of goods for Pharaoh. But birds came and ate them. Joseph said the chief baker's dream meant in three days the Pharaoh would cut off your head and then impale your body on a pole, and then birds would come and eat of your flesh. Imagine hearing that news? The chief baker must have been sad. Pharaoh's birthday came three days later and had a banquet for all his officials. The cupbearer got his job back but the chief baker was killed just as Joseph said. The cupbearer promptly forgot about Joseph.

Two years later Pharaoh had a dream. And in his dream, seven fat cows came up out of a river then seven ugly cows came out and stood next to each other. Then the thin ugly cows ate the fat ones, and then the pharaoh woke up. The Pharaoh wound up falling asleep again and had a second dream. This time he saw seven heads of grain, plump and beautiful, growing on a single stalk. Then seven more heads of grain appeared, but these were shriveled and withered by the east wind. And these thin heads swallowed up the seven plump, well-formed heads! Then Pharaoh woke up again and realized it was a dream.

All night the Pharaoh thought about this and what it meant. So, he called all the wise men and magicians and none of them could tell him what his dream meant. Then the cupbearer reminded the pharaoh about the time he and the chief baker was sent to prison and met a man that interpreted dreams. The Pharaoh ordered they bring the dream interpreter up at once. Joseph shaved quickly, nervous because he was going to be in the Pharaoh's presence. When he got there, the pharaoh asked him if it was true that he interprets dreams. Joseph said that it was beyond his power; however, God will interpret it and set you at ease. So, the Pharaoh told Joseph both dreams.

Then Joseph said that both dreams meant the same thing and God was telling him what he was about to do. He told the pharaoh that seven fat cows and seven plumped heads of grain both represent seven years of prosperity. The thin ugly cows and seven withered heads of green represent seven years of famine. The fact that you had two dreams meant God was going to do it soon. The famine will be so great that the seven years of prosperity will be completely forgotten. Joseph then suggested that the pharaoh find the wisest man in Egypt and put him in charge of a nationwide program and let the Pharaoh appoint officials over the land, letting them collect 1/5 of all the crops during the seven good years. Put them in royal storehouses and store them away. Then when the famine comes there will be enough to eat. otherwise, people will starve.

Then the Pharaoh asked, "What better man to head this operation but you? Since God has revealed this to you, therefore you are the wisest person in the land"! The pharaoh put him in charge of the whole land of Egypt. The Pharaoh also placed his signet ring on Joseph's finger as a symbol of his power. The Pharaoh told Joseph "I, the pharaoh am the king, but no one would move a hand or a foot in this entire land without Joseph's approval". So for the next seven years, there was food all over the land.

Seven years later was pure famine. The famine was terrible and it was everywhere, and only the land of Egypt had food. Now Joseph's father sent his brother to Egypt because they were almost out of food. Guess who they ran into? Joseph! The same brother they tried to kill who is now a grown adult man and now the Prince of Egypt. The brothers didn't even recognize him. Eventually, they did and got scared assuming Joseph was going to get revenge and have them killed. But Joseph said, "It is okay! What you don't

understand is what you meant for evil, God has used it for good!"

What a story that was. I was more concerned about how that pertains to me in my life.

4

Things are not the way they seem

After a few months in confinement, I was released. I was finally able to contact my mother and my sister. They got me a lawyer from Stuart, Florida named Arthur Brandt. My lawyer got my Discovery. The Discovery is a packet of paper that has to entail everything that the state has against you. There can be no surprises of anything that is not stated in the discovery at your trial. Mr. Brandt came to visit me in jail to discuss the case. He told me the state claims to have footage of me making the transaction that caused them to execute the search warrant and make the arrest and we were going to watch it immediately on his laptop.

I was confident they had nothing on me because I cannot remember making any transactions within six months before this, so someone is mistaken. My lawyer opens his laptop and puts the CD in and, what do you know? It is a bright blue screen with nothing on it. My lawyer said the state was bluffing and they did not have anything on me we are officially going to trial. I was high-fiving my lawyer and even jumped in for a chest bump. I knew

I was going to beat this case and I knew God was on my side.

A few months went by, and my faith became stronger, yet I needed more proof from God. He said he would get me out of this I just didn't know how he was going to do it I just believed. So, I prayed for a sign. I just asked God if what you told me in scripture was true, please show me. On this day I was going to court for a docket sounding. Docket sounding is where you go before the judge and they give you a trial date.

In the courtroom that day, my lawyer was speaking for me when suddenly; the lights went out for a few seconds and then came back on. My lawyer joked and said, "Someone must have forgotten to pay the light bill." The whole courtroom starts laughing. But deep inside, I knew it was God showing me a sign. So, I got back to the dorm and immediately called my mother to tell her the good news of what happened and that God had found favor in me.

5 MONTHS LATER

Today was the big day that I was anticipating. I was ready to get this whole thing over with, also with quite a few inmates packed up like sardines in a transport van that was created by an inmate, and it's already designed to seat 10 inmates, 5 on each side with a sheet of metal dividing us. It is so hard to breathe in there, God forbid you are claustrophobic. Legend has it that an inmate created it and sold the model to the penal system and made millions. An inmate creating a device to torture inmates, I would never understand it. I was the first to go in, so I was away from the door. I had to close my eyes the whole ride just to not panic.

We finally arrived at the courthouse, and we were separated into two different cages, one for men and the other for women. Now at this point, I am ready for trial. Between everybody getting everything together including inmates talking to the lawyers or public defenders, it is one big cluster.

I see Mr. Brandt, and he approaches me pulls me into the confidentiality room, and proceeds to say, "Mr. Ackon I have some good news, and I got some bad news." I am shackled hands and feet with a chain connecting both and one could hear the chains shaking. I told my lawyer now is not the time for bad news we are going to trial today. He goes, I understand. "The bad news is, they do have a tape." My heart dropped.

I then said, "You told me they did not have a tape." He proceeded to say, "I know what I told you, however it was my computer, it couldn't read or format rewritable discs. That was what the state gave us to watch." I then began to tell him, "How is that my problem? You mean to tell me that I am about to be screwed over your incompetence?" At this time, I am livid. He then proceeded to tell me, "Wait, before you get upset there is also good news! The state has offered you five years' probation on all 6 charges." With excitement on his face, he tells me I can be out today! I thought to myself but that will mean I will be guilty of all these charges.

I also know this county I am in and this whole state plays a dangerous game. Everything is set up for a trap. I take the 5 years, violate on a technicality (i.e., dirty urine, home a little after my curfew) and that will be it. Whatever time I'm facing will be back on the table. I had a friend by the name of Rolondo in prison right now as I write this from dirty urine. He was in the same boat I was in and took the probation and now doing the full 18 years.

I took a minute to ponder then my lawyer said you do not have to decide right now we are going to watch the tape then you decide what you want to do. The whole time I am praying as the tape starts.

The tape starts with an 18-year-old sub-urban kid getting a camera fixed on his collar to set me up. I recognized as soon as the tape started who this guy was. This guy lived right across the street from me. He was so cool with my kids and also had access through my garage and could walk in, sit down and play video games all he wanted when I was not there. I had a projector that shot the game on the wall which made it wider, and I had put up dark curtains to feel the effects of horror and strategic games. Therefore, he liked being over my house. I later found out that he got caught with a whole bunch of Oxycontin pills and made a deal with the police to set up someone that sells the same thing or equivalent.

This guy is now an informant now? You can see them start to test the video then he and the officer hops in the car and begin to call me at least 25-30 times. I finally answered. But one thing I always despised was talking over the phone. All I said was "come over I will be in the driveway." Eventually, the informant arrives at his house gets out, and walks towards my driveway. My girlfriend and I are backing out of the driveway but cannot be seen on camera.

From his angle, you can see him approaching my vehicle walking from the back of it to the passenger's side where I'm sitting. Ironically, he was singing a hit song by Young Joc called "Dope Boy Magic". It is a song about selling dope and despises informants, which makes it funny that this man is singing this while setting me up. I just laughed to myself about it. I was sitting in the passenger side with my seat leaned back as I told him to come to my side and hop in the back. The back window was up and tinted so the only thing the cameras could see was a reflection of the informant.

I told him to hop in, he said, "No I want to do it right here." Usually, I would sit up, get mad, and say get in the car! But I was in a rush to go at that time, so I handed him a piece of crack through the cracked part of the window, and he handed me 20 dollars. Throughout that whole footage, I was not on that camera once. The only thing you can see is a white hand holding the steering wheel because my girlfriend at the time was driving. It was like those movies where when the character is naked and right when they are about to show a private part a branch pops up to block or something in the background covers them up.

That is exactly how it was. I was nowhere in those cameras. I am willing to take my chance and take them to trial, and that was exactly what I told my lawyer. The judge eventually called my name up and she asked the courts whether we had come up with a decision yet. We say trial. The judge looks me in the face and says, "Mr. Ackon, on count one you're facing 15 years, on count two five years, on count three another 15 years, and one year on each misdemeanor, that's a total of 38 years. Are you sure you do not want to take the five-year probation plea deal?" I said "yes I'm sure."

The judge said "OK we pick jurors Monday at 9 am" and banged the gavel. So, now I was being transported back downstairs to the holding cells in the courthouse. The bailiff walked me downstairs staring at me like I was a statue, as he was in shock. He proceeded to tell me that I should have taken probation. The whole walk consisted of him telling me that the judge's nickname was Hang 'em Nelson, and she would give me the maximum sentence.

He went on to say how he did not care if I was guilty or not and how he would rather be in the comfort of his own home than take a big risk like that. "Please I beg you don't be stupid go back in there and change that plea." I was listening but I was not going to change it but this bailiff was adamant. He pulled me into a different courtroom that was empty just to talk (Which is illegal and a security risk) and told me how he could not stress enough how I needed to go back and change my plea. So just to get him off my back; because now it was to the point he was getting annoying, I said "Maybe if they would have explained it like that, I would have taken the plea." When I got back downstairs, I was handed a brown lunch bag that had a bologna sandwich, two cookies, a mustard pack, and milk.

The correctional officer calls my name before I can even take a bite of my sandwich and says, "Mr. Ackon, they want you back upstairs." So, they put the shackles back on and took me back upstairs. The elevator opens to the holding part of the courtroom. The bailiff and my lawyer are standing next to each other. The bailiff has his hands on his knees breathing hard (and mind you this guy is heavyset). My lawyer says, "Is there something you want to tell me?" The bailiff kept reiterating, "Tell him exactly what you told me, about how you want to change your plea!" This bailiff ran down my lawyer just because he did not want to see me go through that trial! At this time, I was confused, and I forgot exactly what the bailiff and I had already talked about. He again says, "Tell him what you told me."

My lawyer then flipped open his phone and said, "I can call the prosecutor now, all they really want is a conviction, that's it." I was still unsure, and my lawyer saw it in my face. So, my lawyer says, "I tell you what, call me by 6:30 pm tonight and let me know what you decide. If you do not call me, I will spend the weekend getting everything together for trial." I told him, "OK." As soon as I got back to the jail and to my dorm room, I fell asleep.

I woke up when dinner was done, and the trustees were cleaning up the trays from out of the dorm. It is impossible to miss dinner because it is the taxpayer's money that feeds the inmates. So, if you refuse dinner (chow refusal) the CO will have to ask you whether or not you're refusing chow, then mark it down as a refusal. That did not even happen to me. So I woke up seeing the trustees collecting the trays after dinner I jumped up and leaned over the banister yelling to the CO that I did not eat.

He waves me off as if I was trying to scam an extra tray. No time to dwell on that though I must use the phone. There were no clocks there so time with us goes by the times we ate, or what was on TV. I estimated it was about 7pm and I managed to get to the phone, and I dialed my lawyer's phone number back-to-back. No answer. Then, in the back of my head, I remember my good friend Edwin Westby, who has been in and out of the system since young always telling me, "If you are ever in the middle of a trial and you realize you aren't going to win or you cannot beat it, you can always fall back on the last plea deal the state offered you in the beginning because all the state is looking for was a conviction." I saw him telling me this in a bubble caption above my head then the bubble popped. It made me feel better. That whole weekend I was acting like I was leaving Monday. I gave away my whole canteen. I went into cells where they were shooting makeshift dice that were made from toilet paper and stuck in a vent to dry. I received so much love and everyone had some type of positive advice to give me.

Cellmates had mixed emotions. Some happy I was leaving and some were wishing it was rather them. Older men we called "old school", sat me down and schooled me on doing the right thing when I got out. Monday comes, and I am comfortable to the point of cracking jokes in the van early in the morning. People had their own issues, so you can see they were frustrated with me. I did not care, I was going home.

We arrive at the courthouse, and they say, "Mr. Ackon dress out!" Now "dress out" means to put on a suit that has either been donated or brought in from your family members bringing something for you to wear as you go to trial. I yelled, "No I'm taking the deal guys" with a smile on my face. My lawyer says, "No, sorry they took the deal off the table. The prosecutor spent the whole weekend getting the case and everything together so that deal is no longer an option." I had to put the poker face back on, but deep inside I was so sick.

5

This ain't no coincidence

It's time to select the jurors. Jury selection is called "voir dire." It was Monday morning; the tables were flipped to face the jury as I sat down with my lawyer. The prosecutor sat with his assistant on the other side. About 40 regular citizens walked in for jury duty.

My lawyer and I have a packet in front of us that contained all the jury's full names, date of birth, occupation, children's age, background, and if they have been convicted of anything.

It was our job to ask questions like, "How do you feel about cocaine?" "How do you feel about guns?" "Has anyone in your family died of any drugs?" Etc.

The reason for these questions is to see where their head was and whether they would be biased when it comes to the verdict. One thing I realized was all the black people were sitting in the back, and all the "educated" looking old white people were in front.

Each side in the case has a certain number of challenges that can be used without giving a reason. These are called "peremptory" challenges.

Each side may ask the judge to excuse particular jurors. The state has five people they can scratch out for any reason at all, and we have three people we can scratch out. The trick to jury selection is there are only six selected and one reserve out of those 40 people. No matter how many people get scratched or excused, it will never make it to the back. Therefore, all the black jurors are purposely seated in the back. Black jurors do not even have a chance to be on the jury when another black person is on trial, and I am confident that this is done on purpose.

During the questioning, one potential juror was asked a question; he was Juror number 38 on my list. He answered the question with a question. He says, "This man is on trial, and his life is in our hands to decide his fate. All our info is right in front of him. Who is to say this man is not going to come after us or send someone to?" The whole courtroom was stumped, even the judge.

The judge told him, "You are excused." He thanks the judge and walks out of the courtroom. I could not help but think; "Now there is a fantastic way to get out of jury duty."

The prosecutor was James Regan; this prosecutor was very braggadocio and full of prestige. He was completely full of himself and was bent on making an example out of me since I did not take the five-year probation.

With blonde hair and blue eyes, he spoke to the judge as if they were friends. I felt like I had no chance. I looked to my lawyer and hoped for the best. There was always a third seat open next to us, and I just kept imagining God sitting there.

My lawyer objected to everything during trial. He objected so much I had to ask him why he was objecting so much.

He said it is called preserving. In post-conviction relief (If you are found guilty and take it to the higher courts), you cannot argue something that was not objected to in the lower courts. That made sense. So all the objections regardless the judge "sustained" or "overruled," it, is still preserved.

As trial went on my nerves continued to jitter. There is no worse feeling than knowing your life is in the hands of 6 jurors and your fate can be determined that same day. I am praying as the trial goes on.

When they called recess, I was in a holding cell reciting verses that I read and held onto, especially Isaiah 41:10 (fear not for I am with you, be not dismayed for I am your God, I will help you, I will strengthen you, I will uphold you with my victorious right hand.) I had a friend named Nick I knew from the streets.

He was in a different courtroom and was having a trial at the same time, and when recess came, we were put in the same holding cell. We spoke and prayed together as we both were going through this challenging time, but he copped out last minute and fell back on the last plea deal of three years in prison.

He was facing 25 years. The pressure was just too much for him. I thought to myself, "I guess it's just me now."

A few hours later, Judge Nelson called for me as I was sitting in the holding cell. The bailiff brought me to the back room and sat me down.

On the way there, I saw office workers and business-dressed people, and I remember being so excited just to scc actual people from society after being locked up for 11-plus months.

When I sat down, the bailiff said, "Judge Nelson wants you to have this," and threw a slice of cake on the table. It was the judge's birthday. Now I am taking this as a sign from God that he has found favor in me, and he was going to get me out of this.

Afterward, everything resumed in the trial, and the whole focus was on the sale and delivery of cocaine. No one testified about finding any bullets anywhere, not one testimony. Yet the prosecutor describes each bullet and what the bullet does when it penetrates the body.

He went as far as to tell the jury it was their 9/11 patriotic duty to convict this man. Even I knew that was illegal. I was more concerned about why this man was going so hard on me. Even when he presented the evidence to the jury, the little piece of crack rock was the size of a crumb!

The way the jury was shaking their heads said it all as they passed the evidence bag with the rock in it. Now was the time for the jury to deliberate. It took hours as I sat in the holding cell pacing back and forth and reciting every scripture I knew holding on.

A few hours later, an officer walked in and said that the jury had reached a verdict. All I remember thinking was here goes nothing.

I get to the courtroom and the bailiff makes us all rise.

(Jury enters courtroom and the Judge begins to speak) "Go ahead and have a seat. Good evening again, and Mr. Mays, let me just ask you as the foreperson, has the jury reached a verdict as to any of the charges or all the charges? And you don't have to read what it is?

THE COURT: "On some of the charges. On counts one and two, were you still unable to reach a verdict?

MR. MAYS: "No. We haven't reached a verdict on counts one and two (possession of cocaine and sale and delivery of cocaine)"

THE COURT: "Okay, Mr. Mays, if you would hand the verdict to the bailiff, the deputy?

Thank you and the verdict appear to be in proper form, and I am going to ask the clerk to publish the verdict as to the counts that have been reached." "We, the jury, find the Defendant, Bernard Ackon, as to count three, guilty of assault on a law enforcement officer.

As to count four, do you find that Bernard Ackon possessed ammunition beyond a reasonable doubt? Yes. As for count five, the defendant is found guilty of possession of twenty grams or less of cannabis.

As for count six, the defendant is found guilty of the use or possession of drug paraphernalia. So say we all, this 25th day of January 2008." I was speechless.

An all-white jury ages 55 and older just told me that I was guilty of possession of bullets? Not one officer came on the stand and said anything about finding any bullets during the raid. I was stoic.

The jury was then excused, and the prosecutor, my lawyer, and I were asked to approach the bench. All I could hear playing in my head was this song by Joe Budden "My Life." I knew I was going to get the maximum sentence for the bullets.

Anytime anyone goes to trial they automatically give you the max if you get found guilty because you are spending taxpayers' dollars to go to trial, so they automatically hit you.

That charge carries a maximum 15-year sentence. Funny how this was not even the highlight of the case. The case was about a sale and delivery of cocaine that was made on a different day, so how did everything shift to the bullets?

The judge then asked the prosecutor about the other two charges they found a hung jury on and whether the prosecutor wanted to retry them. The prosecutor fixed his blazer with confidence and said, "We will try those two cases again." They scheduled the trial for the same day I was getting sentenced on this case. It was safe to say that my life was over.

6

"Hope deferred makes the heart sick" -proverbs 13:12

The whole ride back to the jail was a state of great confusion. I was so confused that I was laughing to myself. I could not get over the fact that God let me down.

I kept staring at the metal divider in the van that separates the inmates with a million things running through my head. I did not even realize we made it back to the jail so quickly; it seemed like a 3-minute drive when it was a 40-minute drive.

I got back to the Rock Road County Jail with a dejected look on my face. Everyone in the dorm was asking me what happened because I had arrived back so late. It was 11 PM when I got back to the jail. I did not want to talk.

I got to my bunk, picked up the Bible, and slung it across the room on the floor. There is a scripture in the book of Proverbs that goes *"Hope that has been deferred makes the heart sick"* (Proverbs 13:12).

I did not care at that point. God told me He would get me out of this. Every prayer, every scripture I held on to, and now my life is over. Who are you?! You made me look stupid in front of your people and all I do is talk about you!

This is how you play me?? I spoke in such anger. I was so angry that no tears were coming out of my eyes.

One of the inmates walked past my cell and saw me and came in and asked if I was alright. It was a man named Rollington Cox.

This man was significant in my faith because we always spoke about God. We read together, and he was like a mentor to me. I told him I was not OK. Every Bible study, every prayer and scripture all for nothing! He proceeded to ask me for my paperwork and then asked what just happened in court.

He looked at it and then asked me what was going on with these two charges? I said they rescheduled a trial date to retry them at the same time I was getting sentenced for the ammunition.

"It's over for me! My life as we know it is over". He says, "Hey Tribe listen, I do not know about law or anything that is going on but please do me this one favor.

Do not give up on God."

He said that with so much conviction, and I felt it deep within my soul.

I ran so fast to pick up that Bible and ask God to forgive me. I then hopped in my bunk to try to get some rest after that long stress-filled day.

As I have the sheet up about to cover my head my boy pops up in the glass across from the jail. I remember him.

A few months before this situation, this guy used to be in my old dorm. He and his co-defendant did an armed robbery, but he stayed in the car and the other person went in and pulled a gun out. His co-defendant wound up turning on him for less time. We spent most of the time in the same dorm for at least eight months.

Something in my heart told me to write him a letter of encouragement. I do not remember anything I wrote, all I know is that I prayed, and I let the pen move.

I gave him the letter, and after reading it, he appreciated the letter so much he would not stop talking about it. Every day he bought it up. In fact, he wound up going to trial on his case and was found guilty, and they gave him a life sentence. He came back to the dorm with a big smile on his face telling me that it was ok; this letter would get him through it.

I do not even remember what I wrote, but it had to be powerful. So fast forward to now, the same guy I wrote that letter to ask me what happened in court.

I told him I did not want to talk. He continued to throw up sign language because it is impossible to hear somebody on the other side of the jail; we call it the barter system.

He continued to spell words out with his hands, but I could not focus; I was too depressed to read it. I tried to make mouth movements to tell him I was found guilty, and I did not want to talk.

He continued to try to get what he wanted to say out, so I ignored him and as I was trying to put my head under the sheet, he stopped me and told me to wait.

He went to grab something, and he came back, with the same piece of paper, the yellow letter that I had written him, and pointed to it and said,

"Do not forget what you told me." It was then I had hope.

Fast forward to a month later, we finally get back in front of the judge for sentencing. The judge that was on my trial, Kathryn Nelson, was a family/traffic judge because the main judges were switching counties and she was the "fill-in" judge for my trial.

It has been a month since then so now she is back to her family/ traffic courtroom. However, I have to go back to her courtroom to get sentenced and people that are there are normal civilians for basic infractions or family issues.

They saw me walk out with shackles, and the whole courtroom got quiet and looked at me crazy. So, I go in front of the judge. The judge asked if I have any words before pronouncing the sentencing.

It went like this:

THE COURT: "I'm going to let you speak again sir,

Mr. Ackon: "Your Honor, I didn't do anything at all. There's no proof I did anything whatsoever.

You know, they came to the house looking for what was supposedly to be drugs, and they didn't find any kind of drugs whatsoever.

They found a box of bullets, according to what they said.

They found bullets?! Am I going to the Department of Corrections for fifteen years for a box of bullets they found supposedly?"

THE COURT: "Okay, and did you wish to say anything else Mr.

Brandt?" (Obviously, she wasn't listening to a word I was saying)."

MR. BRANDT: "Judge, Mr. Ackon. He's permitted to maintain his innocence, although the Court obviously will and has accepted the verdict of the jury.

There was a search warrant with the full intention of finding a house full of drugs as if this was a drug dealer.

They did not find anything that would indicate that Ackon was a drug dealer, and they didn't find a large quantity of drugs, they found a personal use of marijuana.

They didn't find money, they didn't find anything besides a scale that was on a desk, a work desk next to a computer that could've just as easily been used for work posting mail as it could have been for, you know, not measuring any drugs.

They didn't find any small baggies that would be associated with somebody who was weighing drugs, to package the drugs to be sent out.

They found nothing, and Mr. Ackon maintained his innocence and asked the Court to consider and sentence him to the minimum requirement according to statute. " Once more, she ignored everything, merely passing paperwork back and forth to the clerk without paying attention to anything we said.

THE COURT: "Thank you. Sir, on Count 3, the assault on law enforcement officer, the jury having found you Guilty of that offense, I am going to adjudicate you guilty of the offense, sentence you to serve one year, and credit for all the time you've already

spent. And when were you arrested on that? That was August 16?"

MR. ACKON: "August 17, 2007"

THE COURT: "Of 2007, give you all that credit on that count. On Count 4, possession of ammunition by a convicted felon, I am going to adjudicate you guilty of the offense, and going to sentence you to serve fifteen (15) years in the Department of Corrections. That'll be concurrent with Count 2. Again, you do get credit for all the time you've already spent on the charge.

You will have to pay the court costs of $373.00, the Cost of Prosecution, the Cost of Investigation of $24.00, and $50.00. On Count 5, possession of 20 grams or less of cannabis, I am going to adjudicate you guilty of the offense, and sentence you to serve one year in the County Jail. That'll be concurrent with Counts 3 and Count 4. You will have to pay on that count $125.00 to the Drug Abuse Trust Fund.

Your driving privileges will be suspended for two years. On Count 6, possession of drug paraphernalia, I am going to adjudicate you guilty of the offense, and sentence you to serve one year in the County Jail.

Again, that'll be concurrent with the other counts. So, all of the time is concurrent. You do get credit for all the time you've already spent in the County Jail awaiting trial.

You do have thirty (30) days to appeal the judgment and sentence. Do you have any Questions is Mr. Ackon?

MR. BRANDT: "Judge, Mr. Ackon had asked me before his because you had left out, Your Honor did sentence him to the maximum fifteen (15) years, that I inquire as the court is to the…the reasoning behind that…that conclusion?"

THE COURT: "Okay, I think based upon his prior record, and based upon the testimony that I heard at trial with the officers as far as the ammunition, (But wait. No officer said anything about finding any bullets.) Being a convicted felon, the dog, what was done to the officer, I think that that is an appropriate sentence."

MR. BRANDT: "No other questions."

THE COURT: "Okay and Mr. Brandt is you ready for trial on

Counts 1 and 2? So not only did I just get sentenced to 15 years.

This same day I got sentenced we were about to pick jurors and start trial for the possession of cocaine and sale of delivery of cocaine. God, I am exhausted."

MR. BRANDT: "Yes Judge, we're ready for trial."

THE COURT: "Is the State ready?"

MR. REGAN: "The State is ready."

MR. BRANDT: "Just wanted to speak with Mr. Regan, however."

THE COURT: "Okay."

MR. BRANDT: "...about some possibilities.

THE COURT: "Okay, so we'll go ahead and pick your jury in just a moment sir."

On the way out of the courtroom, I noticed people scrambling to hurry their cases up to get out of that courtroom.

They thought the judge was having a dreadful day when she sentenced me. I don't think anyone who was in that courtroom had seen anything like this.

After all, they were only there for family issues and traffic tickets.

That same day the state came at me offering me a plea saying if I pleaded guilty, they would run the 15-year sentence concurrent with the drug charges that I am about to be retried for, and if I didn't take it the state was going to go after my kid's mother because in the footage of the sale my kid's mothers' hand was on the steering wheel.

The timing of that offer was unfortunate. I was so mad at her for leaving me like this it did not scare me one bit. She left me for dead and was now dating the neighbor's older brother.

I told them to go get her with no hesitation. The prosecutor was upset that it didn't work.

7

This is a man's world

The second trial had everything the first trial had. At this point, I was so exhausted mentally and physically.

I had just finished a three-day trial, found guilty of possession of ammunition by a convicted felon; the judge sentenced me to 15 years in the Department of Corrections on the charge.

The same day, here I am on another trial from the previous trial in which the outcome was a hung jury. All I could think to myself was,

"Here we go again." The trial begins.

The difference in this trial was that now they got every officer that was involved in the bust buy. Each officer said they saw the CI approach my vehicle from different angles of where they were sitting and claimed I made the sale.

The court brought out the same TV with a DVD player to play the transaction from the informant's point of view. Also, the detective who jumped back when the dog launched at her testified this time and told the court she was pregnant at the time that the dog bit her. This is completely illegal and an attempt to sway the jury. I was already sentenced to 1 year on that charge, why would they even mention this? The only thing I can think of was they were trying to sway the jury into feeling sorry and making them convict me out of sympathy.

They were doing everything to get this conviction. A photo showed that all she had was a red mark on her shin. If it were a pit bull bite it would not leave a red mark, it would have a bite mark. But it was only a misdemeanor, so I was not concerned about it.

Misdemeanors fall off your record in a year or two, so it is pointless to fight those, especially when you have bigger issues on your plate. The trial lasted the entire day and now it was time for the verdict. The time is now 9:00 pm, and as the bailiff walks me back upstairs to the courtroom, I remember the bailiff telling me good luck. I looked at him and said, "With God, there is no luck."

The elevator door opens to the detain room as we enter the courtroom. Everyone took their positions and my lawyer tried to put his arm around me, and I moved his arm because I did not want anybody touching me at that moment.

The clerk read the verdict. "We the courts the 19th judicial find Bernard Ackon innocent of possession of cocaine and acquitted of sale and delivery of cocaine."

My knees buckled as I fell to the ground. I just knew God had something up his sleeve. So I was found not guilty of the drug charges. My lawyer explained how he was off my case now and this is where I deal with appellate courts, in my district which is the 4th DCA.

This was all new to me. I was only concerned about how I was going to survive in prison. My release date was July 22, 2022.

March 5, 2008, at 3 AM, and the jail is where they call the inmates who are getting on the bus to head to prison. My name is called as one of the many.

We are all put in this holding cell to wait for the bus. There was this one guy we called "Unc" which is short for uncle because he was older than us and he had been to prison 11 times.

He was telling us the do's and don'ts and what we were to look forward to. It was chilling being my first time.

But one thing that he said that stuck with me was a situation about how someone would approach you and leave a honey bun on your bunk.

If that happens do not eat it because someone is going to approach you later about the same honey bun and ask you for it back. Then you would open your drawer full of the canteen and you will have rows of honey buns.

But the person that approached you would say they want the same one you just ate. If you cannot produce it, he would then threaten either violence or coercion."

We all had crazy looks on our faces. I thought right then I was in some real survival instinct. I would die over my manhood.

As we lined up for the bus, they walked us down the hall. I saw one of my closest friends Marty getting booked as I was leaving the jail. He had blood all over his white tee shirt and spots as if he'd been tased. I yell his name to acknowledge him, and he goes "tribe! Where are you going"? I told him going off to prison. "They gave me 15 years". The Correctional officers told us to be quiet in the hallway so I could not talk much, and it was all in passing.

All I heard him say was "man"! Then shook his head. We got on the bus headed to CFRC (Central Florida Reception Center). On the way there we passed by a hospice compound for terminally ill inmates.

We drove over this overhead, and you can look down and see all these inmates who do not have much longer to live. Wow. These inmates are going to die here, made me think of myself.

I will be 41 when I get out in 2022. What if I die there? I will die alone. It was a three-hour ride there and the whole time I noticed a few adolescents that would rap loudly and beat on any object that could produce a sound and they would rap.

The lyrics were all violent and I could tell that they were young. One person in the middle row yells "We all have issues we are dealing with and now isn't the time for that"! One of them got mad and told him to "shut up or do something about it"!

The bus got quiet, and they picked up where they left off rapping. I just sat there with my mind going 100 miles an hour not knowing what to expect when we finally arrive.

Upon arrival, the officers made us stand side by side in a row beside each other. I noticed one of the inmate's duties was to assist the staff and bring them whatever they needed.

I know that face from somewhere. He nods at me. Oh, snap! It is my boy Isaac from the streets. He used to live in Port St. Lucie with me but then he moved to Orlando and became a bouncer at some of the hottest clubs in the Orlando area like Firestone and Icon off of Church St.

Any celebrity that came through went through him for protection. From Master P to Monica, it made me feel a lot better and I was not as tense anymore. One officer walked up to a random inmate standing in line with us, grabbed him up, and slammed him on the ground.

All the other inmates that got off the bus stared in fear and shock, but the ones that had already gone through these three or four times were not even worried about it. I found out later that it was a scare tactic to instill fear in first-timers.

They eventually walked us all into the reception center. The correctional officer then asks if anyone is in fear for their life and wants to go to protective custody speak now. Oh, remember the adolescents that were freestyle rapping all that violence?

They were the first ones to raise their hands. That entire murder rap was exactly what it was, just rap. Now all of us are escorted through processing. Processing was equivalent to a concentration camp line. We walked in a single-file line getting uniforms, haircuts (completely bald) Medical and DNA swabs. The clothes you came into jail with get assessed, you have to walk up to this section where they box up your old belongings and mail them back home. As I was in that line with my street clothes in hand, I thought about something an old man told me back at the jail.

He said, "Whatever comes with the drug game, goes with the drug game." I was subconsciously trying to prove him wrong by mailing my Jordan's to Clutch's house. I thought to myself this was the last thing I had left from hustling. I lost everything else. I found out later that it got lost in the mail. Wow! That Old Man was right. I had nothing left to show from that era of my life.

Anytime you know you are going to prison it is common knowledge to stack up on stamps because stamps can be used as money in there.

You can get cigarettes, canteen, clothes or whatever in there with stamps. I made sure I saved all my stamps from jail. I did not have any family to help so I had to make a way for myself. Finally, they called chow.

When we get there, we are allowed three minutes to eat. The CO's yell, "Suck it down and get up!" If you are caught eating after the three minutes is up, the COs will take your tray and throw it out. Then there is recreation (REC). Everyone just plays basketball, or they go by the ping-pong table and rap.

There are huts we all stand under, and letters everyone wears along with their numbers. For instance, I'm from St. Lucie County, so our letter is "K" and my number was K74136. Now where the "7" is can change depending on how many times you have been to prison.

If you have been to prison twice it changes to the letter A.

So, say I have been to prison 4 times my number would be KC4136. There are people in there with a J letter. That means they have been to prison 11 times!. Had I been to prison 11 times my ID would have said KJ4136.

That was the letter the one inmate who was preparing us for what we were about to go through in the holding cell back at the jail had. That is crazy! All the "k" stay amongst ourselves most of the time under a hut. Orlando and Tampa had "x" and so on.

I was cool with everyone except this guy named George. He's always asking for stuff but when his canteen comes around and you ask him for something he will not give you anything. It used to peeve me.

Outside I finally had a chance to link up with Isaac, the guy I saw when we initially got off the bus. I hung out with him a lot because we used to hang with the same people on the streets, so we had more in common.

Isaac's story was interesting. He had an issue with his girlfriend, and he had allegedly broken into her home to destroy her clothes. Allegedly, someone saw him breaking into her apartment and called the police. They arrived and Isaac,

Seeing that he was stuck, and having a gun on him, decided to threaten to kill himself. The situation caused people in that complex not to go to work and even kids not to be able to go to school. The irony of it all is that another close friend of ours named Mike was on the phone with the hostage negotiator passing messages back and forth. He finally surrendered and wound up getting 4 and a half years plus deportation when his time was done.

Now I wind up in prison with him, in a small world. He used to tell me all the stories about the celebrities he did security for, and I could attest to plenty of stories because he and another friend named Rohan used to invite us to those clubs and we would not pay a dime for anything.

A lot of COs knew him based on the whole club scene and being that the reception center was in Orlando. They used to give him magazines and he would sell them on the pound. Dirty magazines were called "f*ck books,"

And he will rent them out to inmates for canteen items. That was a good hustle.

People will pay top dollar. Also, the CO's will bring him KFC, McDonald's, etc.. We always used to talk about God body knowledge, 5% knowledge, and things like how Egyptians built the pyramids and conspiracy theories and passed knowledge back and forth.

It is important to know that the reception center was only for "reception." In other words, everyone who goes to prison is sent there till they are sent to their permanent camps.

You are given a "TABE" test and depending on how you do it determines which camp you go to. I aced mine and got a 12.9. But at the time I did not know it played a factor in which camp they sent you to. I did not care. What determine your camp are your charges and your record if both of these are unfavorable, you will be sent to a facility without a law library.

After chow, I used to see the youths marching with red hats. I found out that when you are an adolescent you are forced to march everywhere on the pound, and you do not get to do a lot of stuff. Still three minutes to eat but they are always locked down and come out for about an hour.

But these juveniles are always fighting and stabbing each other, and they are highly creative when they make knives, 90% of them are serving life sentences for their crimes.

At night I used to read a lot mostly the Bible and anything of self-help like the 48 Laws of Power or the 33 Strategies of War by Robert Greene. I used to talk to my bunkie about what I wanted to do when I got out.

He used to laugh at me saying how he was only doing three years and being that I have 15 years, now was not the time to be thinking about that.

I always had hope though. God has saved me through and through and I knew that he would make a way. One day I was on my top bunk and he was on the bottom and I told him this invention I was working on.

After I told him he said, "I appreciate that idea I'm going to use that!" I was in total shock and laughed, hoping he would say he was just messing around with me. But I knew he was serious when he said, "I knew there was a reason why I came to prison!" It was a harsh reality check but I learned that day to keep my ideas to myself. I never spoke to him again.

A few months later the day finally came to go to our permanent camps. It was 3:30 AM and they had about 60 people this particular week headed to their permanent camps.

Another bus ride, but this time it was only an hour 30 minutes and this camp is called Marion Correctional Institution (MCI). I was the last name they called to go to this camp because everybody else was being shipped to Tallahassee, the panhandle. The top left corner of Florida.

To put it in perspective, they were going so far up Florida that if you were standing by the gate of the prison there, you could literally throw a rock and hit the state line of Alabama.

Glad I did not go there. Come to find out Marion was one of the best camps in Florida. Minimal stabbings and it had an exquisite law library. After going through the process, I grabbed my belongings and went to my dorm.

The dorms resembled a tunnel with rooms on each side kind of dungeon type. If you looked outside, you could see the yard.

The yard was huge and you could see all kinds of people outside running, working out, shuffleboard playing, baseball, basketball, and even sections where people were having church. Some were having gang meetings like the Aryan Brotherhood, Bloods, Crips, etc. Safe to say everything was going on in the yard. My roommate hopped off the bunk and began to explain how whenever you see a homemade plane going up that's John Travolta's.

He lives around the corner from here. He asked me my name and I told him Tribe. He said his name was City X and he was from the Bronx but he lived in Tampa. We became cool because we shared the same interests like rap current events in hip-hop and video games.

Hung with him mostly, he was doing eight years for a robbery charge he copped out to in Tampa. I had to get myself a hustle being that I had no family sending me anything.

We have a lot of games in our day rooms in each dorm I always had a thing for words. They had a Scrabble board with two dictionaries specifically for Scrabble, the third and the fourth edition Scrabble dictionaries.

No one touched the Scrabble dictionary so I would take them to my bunk and study the hell out of them. I used to play the best of them for canteen and that is how I fed myself in there.

But prison had a lot of talent. There are people locked up better than Michael Jordan and paint better pictures than Picasso. But they all have high prison numbers and will never get to display their talent. Some of the most skilled hackers, as well as some of the least, were reputable individuals.

8

How did I get here?

Behind these walls, really have you thinking about your life and how you got here. I laid on my bunk when the lights were out and reflected on who I was and how I got here.

My mother and father are both from Ghana and moved here to The United States. They lived in Dallas, TX, and had my older sister there. Then my mom got pregnant with me. My dad was abusive towards my mother, so she took a trip back home to Ghana and had me there while she was pregnant. She was so traumatized by the abuse that she took a whole bunch of pills just to try to end her life.

As a result, she went to the hospital, and I almost died in her stomach. It was then my mom began calling me a miracle baby.

When I was two years old, my mom decided to come back to the States, and at this time we lived in East Orange, NJ.

School was hard for me because I always got into trouble. Even through the abuse, my dad stayed on the bottle. At 9, my mom couldn't take us seeing the abuse, so she got on a plane with me and my sister and went back to Ghana.

We went to live with my mother's brother George, and he had five kids there. A month later, my mom gets on a plane and leaves us there. I was too young to understand why she would do something like that. I later found out that she was going through a divorce and she didn't want us to witness it.

Talk about a culture shock. In Ghana, everyone was older than me and was allowed to discipline me. I was the "hard-headed American boy", so you can imagine how bad I got beaten. It was daily.

I was forced to learn my multiplication tables, and if I messed up, I would be whipped with a cane. Then I would get home, and my uncle's wife would beat me.

My uncle was a flight attendant for an airline in Ghana, and when he got home, he would also beat me. It was an ongoing cycle. It was for anything.

For instance, I wrote a girl named "Abena" a love letter, and I got the same cycle of beatings. That family was so strict.

They followed some kind of 7-day/7-seal religion where they believed a man named William Branham was some kind of reincarnated prophet.

No one wore earrings; no woman wore makeup or anything like that. They had so many strict rules. Now mind you, I am coming from New Jersey running around with my friends, having snowball fights, and riding dirt bikes through trails.

My dad sent me a Nintendo set, and it just sat there for years unopened because I wasn't allowed to play it.

I even had a bike, and I was never allowed to ride it. When I turned 12 years old, my mom decided to have us back. I couldn't be happier. I didn't care to pack anything; I just wanted out of that prison. We arrived back but noticed my mom had moved to Carteret, NJ, while my dad was still staying in the building in East Orange, NJ.

I wondered what was going on. Oh, that day, me and my sister left, the family opened the Nintendo and played it every day; they even rode our bikes daily.

July 25th, 1992, was my first day back in the US. It was hard trying to adjust after three years. I spoke really funny, had a Ghanaian accent mixed with an American accent, and I just couldn't fit in. I was kicked out of different schools for fighting. Even went to a vocational school in Perth Amboy, NJ, and got kicked out of that one.

Eventually, my mom gave us an ultimatum to either go stay with my aunt in Canada or my aunt in Florida. All I was thinking was Disney World and palm trees. We begged my mom to go to Florida. Florida was beautiful.

The town I moved to was Port Saint Lucie, and there was really nothing to get into except a mall. So I met some friends and began smoking weed, drinking, and skipping school.

One day we were skipping school, exploring the backwoods, and my boy Kyle said, "Bernard, you need a nickname. Since you are from Africa, we're going to call you tribe." That name stuck with me ever since.

Being that there was nothing to do; we used to find something to get into. The crowd I ran with fought all the time and did robberies. I guess it's true, birds of a feather flock together. We even fought each other when we had no other crews to fight. Then the arrests began.

Weed charges, trespassing, battery, etc., that caused me to go to programs and detention centers. My mom made me go live with my dad back in New Jersey.

Then I would give him hell, and he would send me back to Florida. It was in increments. Like two years in Florida, three years in New Jersey, six years in Florida then back three years in New Jersey.

It was New Jersey where I got into selling crack for a profit. I eventually came back to Florida and brought the same hustle with me. This is where I kept running into Detective Brieske.

He pulled me and my girlfriend over about a fake warrant, and then my girlfriend, who was pregnant at the time, went into labor. She was flown to Saint Mary's Hospital in West Palm Beach, and she had my son, David, 26 weeks early.

I was released the same night, and my son was born one pound and 15 ounces, the size of the envelope. He was hooked up to a whole bunch of wires, and the wires were hooked onto an apnea box. There were times the box would go off because I thought his heart stopped, and I would jump up out of bed over a false alarm. 2 years later I had my daughter, Taraina, and I thought for sure she would change me. I was in love the moment I saw her. However I never stopped hustling. Having a daughter only gave me a reason to hustle harder and provide so I continued to hustle then came all the troubles. But for some reason, God had a different plan for me. So many situations that God would save me from that could have destroyed me. For instance, I once got a call from someone I was supposed to bring $300 worth of cocaine to; apparently, this person was already in the police interrogation room talking about setting me up.

I received a call that I never responded to, and it went straight to my voicemail, and when that happens, I usually don't listen and I just delete it when it sounds like people talking in the background. At a particular time, this friend was in an interrogation room describing my car and where we would meet every week.

I was in shock when I heard this then you could hear the deep voice man saying, "Well, we are going to see if he is an easy target and we'll see about getting you probation." She then says, "What are we aiming for here, 300? Ok guys, see you on... end of message, to delete press 1 to save press 9." I listened to this message over 100 times to make sure I was hearing what I was hearing.

The only conclusion I could have come up with was she must have accidentally reached into her purse hit the call button and called me, and it went to voicemail. It's the voicemail that picks up the convo. Whatever happened shook me. It was time to clean up the house after that. Up to that moment, I had been raided twice, and I was at the point where I didn't even care anymore.

I don't want to paint the picture like I was this big drug dealer. I did what I had to do to eat. But once my son came into this world, I changed the way I was living. It took some time to stop the addiction, but with the help of my baby's mother, I slowly stopped. Now I'm here, reflecting on my life and thinking about the future.

I just pray I get to see it.

9

Only the strong

Every day except weekends at 11:30 AM before chow, the C.O. will get on the intercom and say, "The following inmates line up for legal mail window."

Most will get silent and listen for the names but those who know they have nothing coming back continue talking.

There are people here who have exhausted all their remedies. The state calls it "throwing everything but the kitchen sink".

Some inmates have filed every motion possible and everything has come back denied so now they are stuck with the time they were given. However, they have acquired so much knowledge from their research that they can get you out, but not themselves. We call them "jailhouse lawyers."

That feeling must be hurtful. Yet there are still some that have been in here 26 years or better just hoping their name gets called for that legal mail window.

I paid it no attention I was just ready to eat at this point I couldn't care less, 15 years. I don't even know if I will be alive by the time I am released. I found myself in the box a lot, mostly for fighting or dumb things like being in the wrong dorm because I wanted to hang out with my boys, or random stuff. So, this particular time I go to the box for skipping the line trying to eat twice.

They gave me 60 days. My cell was next to a guy named Van. This guy had a death wish in prison. He owes everybody in the yard and he purposely borrows and does not pay back and he is only living because no one wants to do anything to him, and plus he is short, like 5'1.

What is crazy about it is he is from St. Lucie County. Every time I have hung around this guy I unintentionally get into some trouble. One time he came into my room just to talk, and 15 minutes later he had left.

Two guys walked past my room and said, "If we find out you're the one with the weed we're going to have a problem." and the guy walked off. I was sitting on my bunk writing a letter when this happened.

All this because I was talking to Van. I was so mad I waited for about five minutes and got up and went down the hallway looking for that guy.

I saw him in another person smoking a joint at the end of the hallway. It was tunnel vision for me; I wanted the guy that said that to. He saw me coming and stood there. I just let him have it and the other guy that was with him hit me in the back of the head and ran. The officers saw it on camera and rushed in. So I was in the box, then a few days later Van came in for a different reason, so we all wind up in the box together, and he met two more people from Orlando and they got cool with each other. When we got out of the box it was January. Every Christmas the chaplain gives every inmate a bag of candy which is worth about $50-$60 in the yard.

Van and I were working outside ground for work and Van had a debt to pay off. I felt bad for Van and I don't know how he did it, but he convinced me to give him my bag of candy and he was going to give me 20 packs of rips that week for the bag. Days passed and it was always an excuse of why he couldn't pay me.

Every time I saw Van in line I asked for my rips, and I was always told he had to go get them and he would be right back. This turned into weeks, and it got to the point that I just had to accept the loss, but the problem is that we are in prison so if anyone were to find out that someone got over on you it could be detrimental.

That will mean 1700-plus inmates on the pound will try me the same way. It was a tough decision. My pride had me in tears at night over this situation knowing I had to do something, but I was not going to.

Then one day I was in the chow hall I had just grabbed my tray on my way to sit down. I observed Van from the corner of my eye talking to somebody, and I heard him tell another inmate how he was going to pay them 50 packs of rips.

I walked up to Van with my tray in hand and asked what about my rips because it's been over two weeks. He then says, "What?! What?!" and he gestures toward me as though he were attempting to start a fight.

At this point, I am looking around and I see the whole chow hall, at least 600 people staring to see what I will do. Then no more than 6 feet from us there is a police officer standing there just waiting for something to go on.

Van knew that the police officer was standing there which is why he did it. In prison that moves is called a "check in" move.

That is when you know the police are standing there (in or around the vicinity) and you become bold because you know they will save you. Everyone stopped eating to stare at us, as if a record scratched, utensils dropping, everyone wondering how I would react.

I yelled with my blood boiling, "Meet me at the yard!" There was no question in my mind that this man was a walking dead man. If there's any time in my life that I was going to take a life, it was right then, because the way everyone was looking at me I had no choice but to make an example out of this one person. I sat down with my tray and one guy asked, "Are you going to eat the rest of that?" I nodded no and everyone grabbed an item off my tray.

I knocked on the table and got up. (Knocking on the table is custom in prison it notifies everyone that you're getting up because in the 60s the tables were never sturdy and they wobbled. it was always four to a table.

So when one person lifts their tray up all the rest of the trays on that table will fall over. So the knock indicates that I'm picking my tray up so everybody else needs to pick their tray up). I walked to my dorm got dressed up for recreation and sat on the bench till they called for rec.

My boy city came and sat next to me and asked, "You're going to do it aren't you?" I was so angry I could not speak. They called on the intercom "Lineup for "Rec" and I was the first in line.

Everyone proceeded outside but I was walking so fast I wind up leaving the whole line behind Just to get to the yard faster.

The C.O. yelled my name and made me realize I was walking too fast, so I apologized and came back to the line.

We got to the "Rec" yard and I saw Van sitting at the dip bar talking to the same person he was in the box with. All I saw was tunnel vision when I approached him, a focused circle while outside of that circle was blurry.

He hops off the dip bar and proceeds to say "What's up Tribe", in a friendly way and stuck his hand out for me to shake it. I learned a lesson within that split second.

When you have a problem with someone the other person is not as focused as you are. You may be burning with rage but it is all inside of you and only you. The other person you are angry at is just carrying on life joyfully.

Anyway, that was just for a split second. I hit the van with everything I had in me the man flew back. I jumped on him, held his neck, and bashed his face. The other guy sucker punches me.

This is where City X came out of nowhere and punched the guy that punched me and an out brawl ensued because others were coming to the rescue of others.

When all the smoke cleared, I was the only person to go to the box.

Here I go again, off to the box, and this time was 90 days.

10

Ignorance is bliss

I finally got out the box and went to the library the same day. The library was split in two. One side had regular books/magazines and the other half had law books. The law library was very clean and had inmates working there running it.

These inmates have pressed prison clothes on because they can afford to. They are millionaires because people send them money into accounts on the streets to help their family members fight their loved ones appeals and cases. They are rich; the only problem is they can only spend $75 a week just like the average person. It does not matter how much you have when you have four life sentences.

I was in the magazine section reading an OK! Weekly magazine that had Angela Jolie and Brad Pitt on the cover, talking about a break up. I put down the magazine and then proceeded to the law section. I was greeted by a man named Mr. Baker. He firmly shook my hand and stared me in the eyes as if he saw something within me. While staring he told me, "I know exactly what you need", and walks back to the shelf and pulls a book out. Now the only places I have ever seen these books are on attorney commercials "Hi you need a lawyer call? Kellerman & Hoskins at 1800..." Those books behind the lawyers are called Florida Statutes and case laws. Case laws are laws that are made from people who fought cases and won (or lost) and new laws get implemented and named after the person who won the case.

Needless to say, I pulled up a chair and read a little bit of it then handed the book back. Mr. Baker then says, "There's no excuse for ignorance of the law." I asked for a few more and just scrolled thru them then went back to my dorm.

The next day I went out to the "Rec" yard. We had options, you could either go to the rec yard or go to the library and I chose the rec yard because that is where my Boy City X was, we walked a yard and I accidentally kicked over an old man's shuffleboard piece.

The old man got up and said, "Young man you kick my shuffleboard piece." I always had a feeling I was going to die in prison, so I constantly had a chip on my shoulder. Something told me to tell this man, "What are you going to do about it?"

But he was old so I just apologized. We wound up sitting with him and having a deep conversation with him. Come to find out that this man has been transferred from camp to camp and this was his 16th camp. He was doing life for murder, and the reason he has been all over was because he was habitually stabbing inmates at every camp he has been. The man has 16 bodies under his belt and that's just in the penal system! They called him "killa". At 63 years old He is a well-known killer in the yard, and no one messes with him, nor does he bother anyone. All he does is play the shuffleboard.

Another lesson learned, treat everybody with respect because you do not know who you are dealing with. What if I had snapped on him? I would not have made it another lap around the yard.

I told City what happened in the law library. He told me I should focus on more on fighting this case and try to give that time back. I was fortunate to filed the appeal within 30 days of my conviction (technically my lawyer did). So I am still within my timeframe.

The next day, I am sitting on my bunk when I hear, "The following inmates' lineup for legal mail window." I hear this all the time, and my name never gets called, plus I did not file anything; that I remember anyway. However this particular time my name got called along with other inmates. So After chow I stood in line. It was a pretty long line, about 30 people standing in front of what looked like a house third-grader kid drew up and it had a door and the window next to the door. A mail lady checks our ID tags and hands us paperwork one by one. What really got my attention was the way every person in that line had their own story. Everyone was silent and had an anxious look on their face. No overhead, and it was raining that day and inmates had their paperwork wrapped in trash bags. Everyone standing in that line in front of that window, had a hope of something good coming from the courts.Nothing expected, Just hoping something breaks through in their cases. Every one of them had a story.

It was my turn to get my mail. It was a letter. I Went back to my dorm to open it and it was a packet from the fourth District Court of appeals (DCA). Cary Haughwout and Dea Abrahamschmitt. This letter from the appellate lawyers saying my appeal is being worked on and any help I can give them will be helpful. This is what made me finally leave the yard life alone and lock my head into the law library.

11

The process

Let me break down the appellate process. It is every person's God-given right to file an appeal. The fourth District Court of appeals is bombarded with appeals. There are people that are red-handed guilty, and they know that they are, yet they will still file for appeal like it is a draw of the lottery But little do people know that the appellate courts do not investigate the evidence of the case. It only looks at the etiquette of the court (Did they say this right? Did they do this right? Was anything illegal said? Etc.) and to make it even harder, if your lawyer does not object in the lower courts you cannot argue it in the proceedings of your appeal.

You would have to file a Post Conviction Relief (PCR) motion called 3.850 (ineffective assistance of counsel) to have the courts look at why it was not objected to. If that motion gets granted, you still would not get out. All they will do is send the case back to the lower courts to be retried, but if the prosecutor chooses not to, then that case gets dismissed.

So, to stay on the topic of appeals, again, the appellate courts get at least 10,000 appeals per day, so they skim through it like "this one has no merit, this one also has no merit, and neither does this one." So, for them to pull a file from an appeal and say, "Hold on, we see something in this," and put it to the side for further review is miraculous and highly not optimistic.

You have a better chance of throwing a wedding ring into a river and hooking it out with a fishing rod.

My whole prayer life was asking God to overturn my case through an appeal, but that was asking God to do the impossible. I know God is a God of impossibilities, but I also have to prepare for post conviction relief. You have a two-year window to file this and if you allow that time to lapse Your chances would be small to get post conviction relief. Therefore, I needed to get started on that now, but still continue to pray and have faith that my appeal will be granted.

So I started reading the Florida Rule of Criminal Procedure. This was the same book that Mr. Baker handed me when I first walked into the library. The book detailed ways to bring the case back to court, and one of them was to file ineffective assistance of counsel (IAC) (3.850). All the mistakes that were made and evidence that was not bought up and failures to object fall under the incompetence of your lawyer. If your argument has merit, you can bring the case back for a new trial. But that could take up to three years for the courts to decide. and there are so much in between that like evidentiary hearings, responses back-and-forth from the courts, etc.. Also, to write a well written 3.850 takes up to a year to research and write up. So I took a few weeks to thoroughly review and dissect everything that happened during my first trial. I noticed so many prosecutorial misconducts the state attorney committed. I began spending a lot of time in the law library, more than I spent in the yard; some evenings I go to the multi-purpose room. Just not on Tuesdays. The pound call calls that "ladies night", because thats where the homosexuals meet up from other dorms to chill and chat. I had a friend name Antoine that was not gay but talked very feminine. I had to pull him to the side and cut him off one day. It was a very hard decision, but I had a long sentence and he only had 2 years. There was rumors already that began circulating and I would have to deal with this while he was here and when he leaves. I felt bad for cutting him off but I had to look out for myself. I came to prison alone.

Back to the story, this room has books about church-related matters and a TV/VCR with headphones where you can watch old sermons. I watch a lot of sermons from different pastors. One particular message was seven steps to reaching your destiny: ➤ Submission: You must learn how to be submissive. It explained how when people go into the army and the drill sergeant is yelling in their faces, it is not to be a jerk. It is to give you a lesson in submission so that when you're out there in the field and you receive a command, you aren't questioning the command. Submission doesn't mean that you are weak; it means you have power under control. We all possess talent and power, but if that power is not regulated, it can turn into a disaster.

Think about this. When you go outside and look around, you see poles and electricity lines. Those poles have on most of them voltage regulators. They are there to distribute the power to the proper perspectives. Now, imagine those voltage regulators not being there.

All that power from those lines will shoot in many directions and not be directed where it is supposed to be. That's what we need.

A voltage regulator is needed to channel our power and talent towards its rightful focus. Submission is the voltage regulator. A man will take this test repeatedly till they get this correct even if it takes the rest of their life.

➢ Sensitivity: you will never be a great man so you can sense the will of God. God is not playing games where he throws you out in life and you just trying to figure things out. God is giving you exercise and sensitivity. He is training you to be in a situation where you are in the proximity of destiny but cannot tell exactly where you are. You can sense it but not exactly sure where it is. You must keep going, tripping over things, scraping your knees, going through trials where gods not telling you because he is developing your senses.

Now you will be able to pray your own way out of situations and all a prophet can do is just confirm it. People become envious of people's lives because they do not sense the will of God for their lives, and they adopt other people's visions.

➢ Separation: Most men don't have the tenacity to separate, be careful of the company you keep when you start getting closer to your dream. The drugs, alcohol, the friends. You're only getting older. Don't make the mistake of trying to take people places they are not destined to go. You could ruin your own blessing by doing this. Even when Moses had to go up Mount Sinai, his brother asked if he could go with him.

Moses told him to stay with the asses (donkeys). Sometimes you have to tell people to stay with the "asses" because I have to go in the direction of my calling. It's like an elevator that is going up and each floor you stop at is one person's stop. Third floor, 6th floor, and so on till you arrive at the top alone, sometimes that requires eating alone, sleeping alone, doing things by yourself.

➤ Set your own stage: God wouldn't call you to do something without giving you the power to do it. God has been setting you up all your life.

Cutting you loose from people, weaning you out of circumstances, teaching you submission, and preparing you to set your own stage, and everything you need is right in your possession. Everything you have at this moment is all the tools you need.

➤ Sacrifice: You must be able to sacrifice something you love. It will not happen without a sacrifice. A miracle will not happen.

You are giving God things you don't care about and if the sacrifice doesn't move you, how is it supposed to move God?

How badly do you want it and how much are you willing to give up?

➤ Switch: The ability to transition in the middle of the road. Some people don't switch because they have much more tradition than transition. We still do everything like how we are used to doing it and you can't do it that way. You can't put new wine in old bottles. You have to have a new mindset.

God is not going to change your circumstances. He is going to change your mind set in the circumstance that will make you change it.

➤ Substitute: For everything you lost, for every blessing that got away, for every time the devil said it was too late, everything will substitute. At the end of this message the pastor looked at the camera and said I am talking to you and went on with words of encouragement.

That message changed something in me. I didn't look at things the same.

12

Dreams

One of the hardest things to do in prison is change your life (or even attempt to for that matter). I went out to the yard to shoot around a little.

This guy by the name of Zoe wanted to play a one-on-one. Prison basketball is very physical and requires talking a lot of trash. In this particular instance, Zoe had possession of the ball and he backed me up really physically with his shoulder. Felt every impact as he dropped his shoulder and bumped me with every dribble, nothing came out of that.

However, that same night I went to sleep, and I dreamt that I was sitting on the bunk talking to another inmate named Big Sexy. Everybody calls him Big Sexy because he is a heavyset person with all gold teeth and supposedly, he was a pimp on the streets.

In this dream, as I am talking with him, I see from the corner of my eye Zoe come from around the corner, and in his hand was a huge oversized sledgehammer and on the other hand a huge oversized concrete nail. Dreams are weird, I get it, but this one seemed so vivid. Zoe signaled everyone to be quiet.

"

Then big sexy immediately grabbed me and held me down with his knee on my neck. I could not move. Zoe proceeded to put the nail to my head and hit it with a sledgehammer. I can hear the nail being hit as it goes to my skull. Everything felt real. The weird part was I knew I was dead.

I was looking sideways as he banged the sledgehammer repeatedly. I immediately woke up frantically. I hopped out of my bunk and went straight to his dorm. He was playing spades. He slammed his last four cards on the table to symbolize he guaranteed the last 4 books were his in the spades game.

I just charged him and started smashing his face with my fist. He fell then I jumped on top of him and proceeded to punch him. The rest of the dorm inmates pulled me off him. I was lucky no guards came.

That night we spoke and squashed the beef and made goulash. Goulash was a sort of jailhouse burrito with a mix of canteen items. He asked what the reason was that I attacked him.

I told him I had a dream that he killed me. The look on his face said it all. I knew he thought I was completely crazy.

Researching has never been easy. To go to the appellate courts, you must have all your ducks in a row. There has always been a rumor that somewhere in the yard there is a secret book called the Nuts and Bolts. It is a self-help legal guide or an index to any case law that pertains to your case.

They are like cheat codes. The book is a rarity, and it is such a gem that even if you do find it, no one would ever let you hold it. I spent so much time in the law library that I wound up getting a job there.

It was here

I met Filipe. He was also working on his cases and post-conviction relief. The only problem with him was he was a huge doubter. He claims to look at the reality of situations. He vehemently doubts my appeal will go through. He sat me down and told me that it was nearly impossible to get post-conviction relief thru an appeal. I told him I knew God.

He then tells me, "all these

inmates in here and you are the only one"? I just sat. He goes on and says, Do not hang your hat on this appeal; start working on your post-conviction relief and habeas corpus. Then he reaches into his bag and tells me he has something for me that may help, and he pulls out the Nuts and Bolts! It was like light glowed around the book. I guarded this book with my life. It cut research time in half, I was reading so many case laws over the next few months that there was a specific case called Daniels vs. State.

I went to sleep that night and dreamt I met Daniels. It was weird because, in the dream, it was a white guy with those 1800 AD sideburns with an American flag in the background waving as he shook my hand, but I knew Daniels did not look anything like that. He just stared at me while continuing to shake my hand.

After months of intense research and constant correspondence back and forth with the appellate lawyer, I finally have an initial brief submitted. The initial brief is my side of why my case should be either remanded (brought back to court and retried) or acquitted.

If the case gets reversed they rarely give you a new trial, they would just let you go under a vacated sentence.

However, that really depends on the severity of the case. They called my name again for the legal mail window, and I finally got a copy of the finished product that was submitted to the court on my behalf. Here goes nothing. I hopped in my bunk and proceeded to read. I was submitting researched case laws to the appellate lawyers because I didn't trust my life in their hands. No one is going to research the way you would. They just wrote it up professionally.

Argument

Point i: The trial court erred in denying

Ackon's motion for judgment of acquittal and new trial on Count 4 because the state did not make a prima facie case of possession of ammunition by a convicted felon.

Point ii: the cumulative effect of the state's improper comments during the closing argument requires reversal.

Conclusion Statement of the Case

Appellant, Bernard Ackon, was charged by Amended Information with:

Ct. 1 Possession of Cocaine for events occurring

6/5/07;

Ct. 2 Sale or Delivery of Cocaine for events occurring

6/5/07;

Ct. 3 Assault on an LEO, for events occurring

8/16/07;

Ct. 4 Possession of Ammunition by a Convicted

Felon, 8/16/07;

Ct. 5 Possession of 20 grams or fewer of Cannabis,

8/16/07; and

Ct. 6 Use or Possession of Drug Paraphernalia, 8/16/07.

Ackon's first jury found him guilty as charged on Counts 3, 4, 5, and 6, but could not reach a verdict as to Counts 1 and 2. After Ackon's second trial on Counts 1 and 2, the jury found him not guilty on both counts.

The trial court sentenced Ackon to one year on Counts 3, 5, and 6, and to 15 years on Count 4. All counts were to run concurrently. Ackon timely appealed on February 28, 2008.

STATEMENT OF THE FACTS

The parties agreed to try the possession of ammunition by a convicted felon with the other charges instead of severing it off, as is usually done.

This made for a rather strange situation at the end of Ackon's trial. Before the trial began, the State moved to light that ownership of the ammunition was not an issue. The defense agreed that ownership was not an issue, but that knowledge was.

Another issue that came up was the defense claiming that the State had not revealed that Ackon had made an incriminating statement when police executed a search warrant at his home. According to Detective Canady, Ackon voluntarily said that all the police would find was a little pot that belonged to him. At first, the prosecutor said that this statement was revealed at Ackon's bond hearing.

The State had a tape of the bond hearing, but there was nothing about Ackon admitting that he had marijuana in the house.

The defense counsel said that he was

prejudiced because he would have changed his entire trial strategy, including perhaps reconsidering an earlier plea offer - had he known of Ackon's statement about the marijuana. The trial court found that there was a discovery violation, but that it was inadvertent. The violation was substantial, said the trial judge, but it did not affect the defense counsel's ability to prepare for trial, thus began a pattern of rulings adverse to the defense which lasted all trial long.

Detective Janet Palmer, of the Port St. Lucie Police Department, was the first State's witness. Since Ackon was found not guilty of possession and sale or delivery of cocaine, her testimony of the June 5, 2007, events is irrelevant to this appeal.

Over defense objection, Palmer was allowed to testify that police did a trash pull before getting a search warrant of Ackon's home. Palmer was allowed to tell the jury that police found marijuana in Ackon's trash. This marijuana was not the same marijuana found in Ackon's house. Palmer testified that the marijuana found in the trash served as probable cause for police to obtain a search warrant. The search warrant was executed on August 16, 2007.

Palmer said that Detective Canady, Sergeant

Briske, Sergeant Grohowski, Officer Kim, and Officer Horton all were involved in executing the search warrant on Ackon's home.

Palmer said that they approached Ackon's home, knocked on his door, and announced they were police officers. After a reasonable length of time, when no one answered the door, the Police broke down the door and entered the house.

She said that they continued to call out police! as they

entered the house. Palmer opened an inside door from the house to the garage and saw Ackon and a dog. The dog barked and lunged at her, and she quickly shut the door. Palmer went outside and around to the garage. The garage door was now open.

Ackon was casually walking out of the garage. The dog was with him, but not on a leash. The dog came at her, and at some point, it bit her on her right shin.

She was wearing long pants, and the bite mark made a scratch mark on her leg but did not actually pierce the skin. When Ackon saw the mark, he said it looked like a scratch and not a dog bite at all. His remark about the bite was introduced to show how callous and uncaring he was. Over defense objection - again - the State was allowed to introduce the fact that Palmer did not know that she was pregnant at the time she was bitten by the dog. Palmer testified that police discovered a digital scale, rolling papers, less than 20 grams of marijuana and some ammunition in Ackon's house. However, because she was dealing with her dog bite and EMS, she did not know where any of those items were found.

Palmer admitted that no firearm or cocaine was found in the house.

Detective Garrett Canady, also of the Port St. Lucie Police Department, testified that he was involved in the execution of the search warrant on August 16th. After he had entered Ackon's house, he heard Palmer yelling "get your dog! get your dog"! outside.

He went outside where he observed a dog aggressively barking and coming towards Palmer. Canady also saw Ackon standing outside in his driveway. Canady immediately ordered Ackon to get down on the ground.

Canady had Ackon at gunpoint. While Ackon was face down on the ground, he repeatedly asked Canady, "let me get the dog; I can get the dog, let me get the dog". Canady finally let Ackon up, and after a few attempts, Ackon was able to get the dog and take it inside and secure it.

When Ackon had done this, Canady put Ackon in handcuffs and read him the search warrant and his Miranda rights. When the State asked Canady if Ackon said anything to him, Canady answered that Ackon did not want to talk to the police; he exercised his rights.

There was no objection from defense counsel; then the State elicited the admission which had been the subject of the earlier Richardson hearing. The prosecutor asked if Ackon made any spontaneous comments, and Canady testified that Ackon volunteered that the police were not going to find anything except a little bit of pot that was his. Canady said they did find the marijuana, plus a scale, rolling papers, and 27 .357 bullets.

Canady identified photographs taken of a desk in a bedroom of the house. The first photo just showed a computer, some cigarettes, an ashtray, some papers, and CDs or DVDs. State's number 13 was another photo showing part of the desk, some magazines, rolling papers, some marijuana, and cigarettes. The last photo was an overall shot of everything found at or on the desk.

Canady testified that the marijuana was right next to the papers on the desk. The box of ammunition allegedly found in Ackon's house was nowhere in these photographs.

Canady could not recall whether Sergeant Briske or he then took photographs in the house. Canady said that he did not actually collect any of the evidence.

He sat in the dining room and acted as a scribe. The other officers brought the evidence to him, and he made note of it and placed it into evidence bags. Although Canady said he did investigate all the rooms for anything illegal, he could not say where the ammunition was found.

He also admitted that no one brought him any firearms or cocaine. There was no testimony from anyone as to where the ammunition was discovered. Although Ackon was the only person home when the search warrant was executed, Ackon's girlfriend lived in the house with him. Indian River Crime Lab analyst, Babu Thomas, testified that he received State's number 4 (the marijuana) and tested it. The substance was marijuana.

Here is the passage with appropriate punctuation: Ackon tried to ask Thomas whether the digital scale was submitted for him to see if there was any drug residue on the scale. The State objected, saying it was irrelevant and beyond the scope of direct. The trial court sustained the objection, finding that whether or not the labs can test such items as the scale was clearly not relevant to anything.

Defense counsel argued that if a lab could test the scale for residue, but the State did not have it tested, it was relevant as to whether the scale was used for drugs or not. The judge disagreed. Firearms expert, Mark Chapman, testified that he received State's number 5, which was a cartridge box, in his lab for testing. He test-fired one of the bullets to see if it fired correctly, and it did. Chapman said that there were three different types of ammunition in the box. There were (22) .357 magnum caliber bullets manufactured by Remington, with brass cases.

Then there were four .357 magnum caliber cartridges manufactured by Federal which were soft points. Lastly, there was one .357 bullet that was a hollow point.

The defense objected to testimony regarding the ammunition because there was no testimony about where the ammunition was found. The trial court overruled his objection. The defense objected to the State's eliciting testimony from Chapman about the significance of the differences between the various types of bullets.

The defense argued that such information was irrelevant to whether or not Ackon possessed the ammunition, and testimony about the effects of these various types of bullets was prejudicial and totally irrelevant. Defense strongly objected to testimony about how much damage each type of cartridge could cause to a person.

The trial court at one point asked the State:

COURT: What is the relevancy?

STATE: Judge, he is an expert, the only one qualified to tell them the difference between different bullets, if there is any. I don't know what it is.

DEFENSE: Can I ask what the relevancy of there being different types of bullets in there is

COURT: I have not read the instructions on the charge. So I'm not sure at this point.

STATE: Well, Judge, if there are three different kinds of ammunition, I think we need to know if they go in different sorts of firearms or (Indiscernible) they do different things from the same firearm. I guess that

DEFENSE: what's the difference if it does or it doesn't

STATE: That being said, Judge, because clearly they don't come sold like that. We would ask the question as well. That's so- and we just leave it at that. Then

whatever —

[The next exchange between the trial court and the State is indiscernible.]

DEFENSE: I don't see the relevancy if it's not sold like that or is sold like that. He either possessed the ammunition or he didn't possess the ammunition. I don't see what the difference is with the different damage it can cause. (Indiscernible) ammunition or he does not have ammunition. There are no enhancement penalties for different types of ammunition of this nature.

COURT: I'm going to overrule the objection. So he will be allowed to testify to that.

Chapman was permitted to testify that the Remington's were normally used for target practice. They were designed to make neat holes in a piece of paper.

The defense continued to object throughout this type of testimony. Chapman then testified that the soft point was designed to stay together better when striking and "the hollow-point bullet", said the witness, "was designed to expand when it strikes an object and to stay in whatever it strikes". Chapman said that a person would not be able to buy a box of ammunition with different types of bullets in it. He affirmed that all the .357 cartridges could be fired from the same firearm. The jury, which was allowed to ask questions of the witnesses after they had testified, asked Chapman how many bullets in the box were hollow points. Chapman answered, "only one".

The State rested and the defense moved for judgment of acquittal on Count 4, the possession of ammunition count. Ackon argued that the State had presented absolutely no evidence of where the ammunition was found and no evidence that Ackon had any knowledge of the ammunition being in the house. There was not even any evidence that the ammunition was found inside the house since there were officers who were in the backyard. The defense argued that the State had failed to make a case for constructive possession of the ammunition.

As to Count 3, assault on an LEO, Ackon argued that the State presented no evidence that Ackon deliberately released the dog or sicced the dog on the officers. There was no evidence that the dog had a history of aggressiveness or that it had been trained to be violent.

The defense conceded that the State had met its burden of proving a prima facie case on the marijuana and paraphernalia charges, but not to the possession of ammunition or the assault counts. The trial court simply said that it found that the State had made a prima facie case for each of the offenses.

The defense asked the trial court to put into the record what evidence the State thought it had presented to show that Ackon had any knowledge of the ammunition or that the ammunition was anywhere where Ackon should have had knowledge it was there.

The prosecuting attorney made the following statement:

STATE: Your Honor, having done some research last night regarding this, there's testimony from Detective Canady that you only going to find cannabis. He admits possession of the cannabis. Cannabis and ammunition are found in the same room. DEFENSE: Judge, that's never been testified to. The State insisted that Canady had testified that the ammunition was found in the same room as the rest of the contraband. It did admit that the ammunition is not in the photographs taken of the contraband found in that room However, the State proceeded to contend: STATE: And, that being said, the Defendant can be simultaneous- to be convicted under Samuels Commonwealth, which is a Virginia case, Judge, 1995 Westlaw 452 360 - to be convicted simultaneously in possession of cocaine and a firearm, if you establish constructive possession of one, that would attach to both.

So in other words, he admitted that he had the cannabis in the room with the ammunition. Under that premise, "if he's got the knowledge, guilty knowledge science of the cannabis, he has the same knowledge that can transfer like intent to the ammunition". In addition, Judge, in People v. Shadblow from New York 209 2d 1011, direct evidence of dominion and control over an apartment or dwelling despite the lack of direct evidence of dominion and control of contraband is sufficient to prove constructive possession. He was the only person there in the house and nobody else there but him and his canine.

The trial judge replied:

COURT: Mr. Brandt, my understanding of the evidence was that officers on this particular day executed a search warrant. They searched the inside of the house. The following items were recovered; a scale, rolling papers, a small amount of cannabis, and ammunition.

DEFENSE: thats not the testimony, Judge. The warrant is not evidence. Testimony was that he went the only testimony was Detective Canady was the one who said he went in the house. He seized the cannabis and he went outside to get a duffle bag. That's when the officer came back in and that's when he found the ammunition.

I asked him specifically, "Did you take pictures of the illegal items that you found?"

He said, "Yes, I did. Of all the illegal items that you found? Yes, of all the illegal items that were found, that he found. He did not find this."

COURT: "What difference does it make, Mr. Brandt, if Detective Canady found it or if some other officer found it in the house and brought it to Detective

Canady?"

DEFENSE: "Certainly, Judge, there has to be testimony that it was found in the house. For all we know, that item was found in the backyard up against the fence that could have been on either property. It was brought forward, and here it is. That's a reasonable explanation of what could have happened. The trial court said that no one testified that they searched the backyard, and Ackon said that there were two officers sent into the backyard. No one knows who brought the ammunition forward or where it was found."

[The trial court went back to its version of events, concluding that]

COURT: "But my view of the evidence is that the items that were introduced and are in evidence were recovered from the house where the Defendant was the sole occupant when the officers arrived. So - for those reasons - but for those reasons, I am going to deny the motion for judgment of acquittal." DEFENSE: "Just to clarify, the warrant, Your Honor, the signed did not say that Mr. Ackon was the sole resident of the home. The warrant that was signed said there were two residents of the home. And, therefore, to hang our hat on that alone is, I believe, incorrect. Further, judge, and I understand you denying this judgment of acquittal. Certainly, case law does suggest that the jury must be instructed — it has to find — that Mr. Ackon had actual knowledge that — knowledge of possession is an element that must be proven beyond a reasonable doubt.

And without any testimony as to where this was found — for all we know, Judge, this could have been found in a drawer with women's clothing in it that he would have no reason to go to. There are more — there's more than sufficient doubt. There are many different reasonable explanations of where this could have come from. And, based upon that, Judge, The State should not be permitted to proceed.

After this, both sides rested on the record. The State wanted, over defense objection, a principal instruction, and the trial judge granted the request. The defense counsel objected to some of the prosecutor's improper comments during the closing argument. Unfortunately, Ackon did not object to some of the most serious, prejudicial ones. The defense objected to the prosecutor saying, (nothing is suggesting that somebody else owned that cannabis for example the basis for the objection was burden shifting. The trial judge said, I don't see how that's burden-shifting and overruled the objection.

The prosecutor promptly continued by stating: STATE: "As I said, I'm asking you to consider what we have in evidence. And you can also consider the lack of evidence. But you can't worry about stuff that we haven't heard about.

That wouldn't be reasonable. You'd be speculating. It would be — it wouldn't be just. It wouldn't be the law. Defense again objected, saying this was an improper statement of the law. The lack of evidence is to be considered by the jury, argued the defense. It was not right for the prosecutor to tell them they did not need to consider what was not there. The trial court once again overruled the objection. Here are some of the worst arguments the prosecutor made; worst because they completely misrepresented the law:

STATE: "We have several kinds [of bullets] in here.

My suggestion is, is that that's how we know the Defendant exercises care, custody, dominion, and control because we have mixed bullets in here.

Somebody was in here, had their hands in here, and put a cadre of different kinds of ammunition in here. ... How do we know that it's also in his care, custody, and control? Due to the cannabis, we are the cannabis.

Mr. Ackon said all you're going to find, all you're going to find is the cannabis. So he acknowledged that there's cannabis present. Now you are permitted circumstantially to - Well, it's a lot like connecting the dots here and there's a hundred dots and the State has gotten up to ninety-eight, you all can step back and look at the picture. I don't need to put in ninety-nine and one hundred for you all to know what it is. He said all you're going to find is cannabis. Okay? Certainly, admitting to having that would have different consequences than just having this. My suggestion would be that his claiming control of this allows you to infer circumstantially that he also had control of this and this and this, certainly if it's found in the same room where he's doing some sort of work with playing games."

STATE: "And, in fact, you find there may have been another actor; if, in fact, you - hey, what if this is the girlfriend's ammunition? Well, they lived together, and they owned a house together. It can be joint possession.

They can both possess something." "Again, I wanted to go over the constructive possession portion of the law which is something that you might want to consider... I want to point out that the standards for the possession of ammunition are not quite the same as the - of drugs.

So for possession of cannabis - for possession of ammunition, all that the State would have to show is that Mr. Ackon had in his care and custody or control of the ammunition or that he has care, custody, and control of that house. It's his house. Whereas with cannabis or cocaine, there's more of a — It's more of a knowledge, a higher knowledge standard. Again, the State erroneously states that the ammunition was found in the same room with the cannabis!

STATE: "[Ackon] says that's my cannabis. Your - it's allowable for you to - to circumstantially infer that if he's claiming responsibility for this, all the other contraband that's in that area within his care, custody, control is also in his care, custody, and control even though there's no verbal admission concerning that. That's perfectly allowable under the law. And I ask you to consider that theory." Finally, in rebuttal, the State again tells the jury that they can infer that Ackon knew about the ammunition because he admitted he had some cannabis:

STATE: "Well, okay, they did find cannabis. But those words [Ackon's admission about the pot] are important because, according to the law, when somebody - if you don't have direct evidence of control or knowledge of contraband and here - well, and here we have this ammunition - both the target-shooting type and the hollow point which is meant to stay in the body and do damage- mixed into different kinds of ammo mixed in - as you can see, they're different. You have the copper-jacketed ones meant to stay together and penetrate better. The lead point is meant to expand as it enters the body. It's not permissible to have these under certain circumstances. Now how do we know that the defendant knew about it? Is it because there are different kinds of ammo in the box? Because he said he knew about the cannabis? Or is it because that directly indicates his awareness? One of the ways we can tell what people are thinking is if they know about something that's under their control. You can assume

- it's safe to infer - that he knows about this too." The prosecutor then went on again about how the jury could infer that the ammunition was under his care and control because the box had different kinds of ammunition in it.

The defense started his closing argument by saying:

What we started out here was with a comment this is overzealous action. It's excessive law enforcement actions, its excessive actions by the prosecutor's office. it's why we're here today The State immediately objected.

The trial court sustained comments about the prosecutor being overzealous. The defense changed overzealous to jumping to conclusions and did not specifically say it was the prosecutor's office that did the jumping.

However, this led to a bigger issue when the State started its rebuttal argument.

The state informed the jury:

STATE: "It's not often that I get to go into what my role is. But I have an invited response opportunity.

When I filed these charges, I — "

DEFENSE: "May we approach?"

STATE: " — my standard is I can prove these."

DEFENSE: "May we approach?"

Ackon argued that it was bolstering for the State to talk about how he has a good faith reason to file and that he has to prove it.

The trial court responded by saying it thought the defense counsel invited this response when he said the prosecutor's office had been overzealous and jumped to conclusions. The trial judge concluded, (The prosecutor] does have an obligation. A good faith - he has a good - he has to have a good faith basis to file a case. That's part of his responsibility. The defense then argued that if the State was going to say he has certain standards to go by, then it must be clarified that beyond a reasonable doubt is a higher standard for conviction. Otherwise, said the defense, it would be misleading and bolstering for the State to talk about its responsibility in filing charges. The trial court overruled defense objections.

The prosecutor went on:

STATE: "Again, I'll let you be the judge of whose being overzealous and who's jumping around the courtroom. Okay? If I have the opportunity to make an invited response, the allegation is that I'm acting overzealous.

When I file that information, I swear an oath that I can file these charges in good faith. And that's how I proceed. There is no kangaroo court here. There's no conspiracy to get Mr. Ackon." Before the State finished its rebuttal statement, the defense counsel argued once again that the prosecutor's remarks about having a good faith basis were improper. The defense asked for a curative instruction.

At first, the trial judge refused to give a curative, but Ackon insists, saying he will move for a mistrial if a curative instruction is not given. The defense referenced Harris v. State, 570 So. 2d 397 (Fla. 3d DCA 1990).

Along with other cases, to assert that arguments made in good faith are inappropriate. The trial judge and defense counsel argued back and forth about what kind of curative could fix the damage. The trial court pointed out that the words were already spoken.

It was only when the prosecutor said, "In the interest of justice and judicial economy and expediency and fair play, please let Mr. Brandt have his instruction" that the trial court said okay and asked what he would like the court to say.

The defense wanted the curative to say:

The standard of proof for bringing forward charges from the State Attorney's Office is different than the standard of proof required here today for a conviction. And they must follow beyond a reasonable doubt standard.

The trial judge was going to say this until the prosecutor asked, "If you could just say to bring charges I have to have a good faith basis." The defense counsel agreed to that.

So, the curative instruction turned out to be: COURT: "...I do want to advise all of you that to bring charges, the State Attorney's Office has to have a good faith basis to bring charges. However, the burden is still beyond a reasonable doubt. That burden is beyond a reasonable doubt. And the State the State of Florida has to prove that the charges were committed beyond a reasonable doubt." The jury brought back a verdict as discussed in the Statement of the Case, supra. However, another issue came up once the jury found Ackon guilty of possession of ammunition because they were not told that Ackon was a convicted felon.

Instead of having the jury go back and make a finding of whether Ackon was a convicted felon or not after the State presented evidence, the trial judge decided to send the jury home because it was late and make the finding herself.

Ackon agreed to admit that he had a prior felony conviction. No one objected to the trial court arbitrarily deciding to make the determination that Ackon was a convicted felon, to meet the final criteria of the offense of possession of ammunition by a convicted felon.

The trial court swore Ackon in, who proceeded to testify that he had been convicted and adjudicated for a prior felony. The trial judge duly found that Ackon was, in fact, a convicted felon. At the beginning of Ackon's sentencing hearing, defense counsel asked for a new trial, based on insufficiency of the evidence as to the possession of ammunition by a convicted felon. (ST. 3) The defense argued that where possession of a firearm or ammunition might be joined instead of exclusive possession, a defendant's knowledge of the contraband is essential, as is his ability to control the item. Such knowledge and ability to control it cannot be inferred if there was a possibility of joint possession. (ST. 3) defense counsel pointed out that the State presented absolutely no testimony about where the ammunition was found. Nothing connected Ackon to the ammunition except that it allegedly was found someplace in his house.

But Ackon's girlfriend also lived there, a fact that the trial court acknowledged was true. The trial court denied the motion. The trial judge sentenced Ackon to exactly what the State asked for.

SUMMARY OF THE ARGUMENT

The State failed to make a prima facie case of possession of a firearm by a convicted felon where the State failed to present any evidence of where the ammunition was found, whether Ackon had knowledge of its presence, or whether he could maintain control over the ammunition. Without any testimony of where the ammunition was found, the State couldn't prove the elements of constructive possession when both Ackon and his girlfriend lived in the house the police were searching.

The trial court erred when it denied Ackon's motions for judgment of acquittal and new trial. This count should never have gone to the jury because the State's case was legally insufficient.

Additionally, the prosecutor made many seriously improper arguments to the jury. The prosecutor at least twice told the jury that the ammunition was found with the cannabis - an allegation that was completely unsupported by the record.

That was the problem with the State's case on Count 4; a lack of any evidence as to where the ammunition was found. The prosecutor also told the jury that it could infer that Ackon knew about the ammunition, had control over it, and had possession of the ammunition because Ackon admitted that the cannabis was his.

Actually, he told the police all they were going to find was a little cannabis. But the prosecutor told the jury they could use his statement to prove that he must have known about the ammunition, too. Finally, the prosecutor made an improper good faith argument, telling the jury that, as an ASA,

he had to swear an oath that he was acting in good faith before he could bring charges. This was both highly prejudicial and unethical.

The cumulative effect of the prosecutor's improper arguments requires this Court to reverse and remand for a new trial.

POINT 1: THE TRIAL COURT ERRED IN DENYING ACKON'S MOTIONS FOR JUDGMENT OF ACQUITTAL AND NEW TRIAL ON COUNT 4 BECAUSE THE STATE DID NOT MAKE A PRIMA FACIE CASE OF POSSESSION OF AMMUNITION BY A CONVICTED FELON

In reviewing the denial of a motion for judgment of acquittal, a de novo standard of review applies (Pagan v. State, 830 So. 2d 792, 803 (Fla. 2002). Generally, an appellate court will not reverse a conviction that is supported by competent, substantial evidence Id: (Terry v. State, 668 So. 2d 954, 964 (Fla. 1996).

Where a conviction is based entirely on circumstantial evidence, a special standard of review applies to determine whether the evidence is legally sufficient to sustain the conviction. Miller v. State, 770 So. 2d 1144, 1148 (Fla. 2000) (citing State v. Law, 559 So. 2d 187, 188 (Fla. 1989). A motion for judgment of acquittal should be granted in a case of constructive possession where the evidence is wholly circumstantial, and the State fails to present evidence from which the jury can exclude every reasonable hypothesis except that of guilt. Daniels v. State, 777 So. 2d 1113, 1116 (Fla. 4th DCA 2001) (citing Dupree v. State, 705 So. 2d 90, 94 (Fla, 4th DCA 1998).

In other words, the state's evidence is "insufficient to warrant a conviction" as a matter of law, no matter how strongly the evidence may suggest guilt when the evidence offered is not inconsistent with any hypothesis of innocence. Daniels v. State, 777 So. 2d at 1116. (Citing Dupree v. State, 705 So. 2d 90, 94 (Fla. 4th DCA

1998); State v. Law, 559 So. 2d 187, 188 (Fla. 1989).

To prove that Ackon was guilty of possession of ammunition by a convicted felon, the State had to prove beyond a reasonable doubt that:

> 1. Ackon knowingly had in his care, custody, possession, or control ammunition; and

2. Ackon was a convicted felon, Florida Standard Jury

Instructions in Criminal Cases, §10.15. The trial court defined "care and custody" as meaning immediate charge and control was exercised over the ammunition.

The jury instructions for possession of ammunition by a convicted felon state: To possess, means to have personal charge of or exercise the right of ownership, management, or control over an object. Possession may be actual or constructive. Actual possession means:

a) The object is in the hand of or on the person, or

b) The object is in a container in the hand of or on the person, or the object is so close as to be within ready reach and is under the control of the person.

Mere proximity to an object is not sufficient to establish control over the object when the object is not in a place over which the person has control.

Constructive possession means the object is in a place over which (defendant) has control, or in which (defendant) has concealed it. If an object is in a place over which (defendant) does not have control, the State establishes constructive possession if it proves that (defendant) (1) has knowledge that the object was within (defendant's) presence, and (2) has control over the object.

Possession may be joined, that is, two or more persons may jointly possess an object, exercising control over it. In that case, each of those persons is considered to have that object.

If a person has exclusive possession of an object, knowledge of its presence may be inferred or assumed. If a person does not have exclusive possession of an object, knowledge of its presence may not be inferred or assumed.

Florida Standard Jury Instructions in Criminal Cases, statute 10.15. The State certainly did not prove actual possession of the ammunition. Although there was no testimony as to exactly where the ammunition was found, surely the State would have made it known had the ammunition been found on Ackon's person or within his immediate reach.

Thus, the State had to prove constructive possession, but it failed to do so. Undersigned has not found a Florida case where the state has convicted a defendant of possession of a firearm or ammunition by a convicted felon where the state did not present any evidence of where the illegal item was found.

The situation in the instant case is unique in this respect. To prove constructive possession, the state must prove elements such as knowledge and ability to control, and whether the item was in the defendant's exclusive possession or whether the possession was joined.

All these elements are virtually impossible to prove without knowing where the illegal item was discovered.

The only thing we know in the instant case was that it was allegedly found during the execution of a search warrant for Ackon's house.

Ackon's girlfriend also lived in the home.

Defense counsel was right when he said, for all anyone knew, the box of ammunition could have been found outside or in his girlfriend's underwear drawer.

Without knowing where the ammunition was found, it is impossible to determine whether or not Ackon had exclusive possession or control of it.

Under the circumstances in this case, the fact that two people lived in the house argues against any finding that Ackon could have had exclusive possession of the ammunition. See (Coley v. State, 393 So. 2d 60 (Fla. 3d DCA 1981).

(When the sawed-off shotgun was found underneath Coley's and his girlfriend's bed, Coley did not have exclusive control over it).

As pointed out in the Statement of the Case, supra, defense counsel cross-examined Detective Canady about whether he had taken pictures of the illegal items that he found during the search.

Canady admitted that he had taken photographs. But when defense counsel tried to get Canady to say where the ammunition was found, Canady refused to answer.

Although Ackon did not specifically request the photographs, Ackon did ask Canady if the photographs showed the illegal items that Canady had found.

Again, Canady said that they did. Without knowing where the ammunition was found, it is impossible to say whether Ackon could have exercised care, custody, control, or management over the ammunition.

Because the State did not present any evidence of where the ammunition was found, the trial court erred in denying Ackon's motions for judgment of acquittal and new trial. This count should never have gone to the jury because the State's case was legally insufficient.

POINT II: ACKON'S CONVICTION SHOULD BE REVERSED BECAUSE OF THE PROSECUTOR'S SERIOUSLY IMPROPER ARGUMENTS TO THE JURY.

The prosecutor made numerous seriously improper arguments during the guilt phase of Ackon's trial. Many of the arguments misstated the law and all of them were highly prejudicial.

The cumulative effect of the prosecutor's improper arguments requires this Court to reverse and remand for a new trial. The prosecutor made several erroneous statements of the law.

For example, the prosecutor told the jury that the possession of ammunition count had a lower standard of proof than the possession of a controlled substance.

Ackon is correct when he argues that the prosecutor misstated the law when he told the jury that it could infer that Ackon had knowledge of the ammunition simply because he admitted to having cannabis.

In addition to these serious misstatements of the law, the prosecutor made highly prejudicial comments about Ackon during his rebuttal closing argument.

The prosecutor twice told the jury that Ackon was the one who said that the ammunition was found with the cannabis, but there was no evidence to support this statement.

This misstatement of the evidence prejudiced Ackon and requires a new trial. The prosecutor also made a highly prejudicial "good faith" argument when he told the jury that he could not bring charges against Ackon unless he had a good faith basis for doing so. Ackon is correct when he argues that this argument was improper because it told the jury that it could rely on the prosecutor's good faith in bringing charges against Ackon.

In conclusion, the prosecutor made numerous seriously improper arguments during the guilt phase of Ackon's trial. Many of these arguments misstated the law and all of them were highly prejudicial.

The cumulative effect of the prosecutor's improper arguments requires this Court to reverse and remand for a new trial.

The officers got the two men out of the car and searched the car and the trunk. They found a 45-caliber handgun on the floor, some 22 caliber bullets in the glove box, and a shotgun, rifle, and more ammunition in the trunk.

The car was a rental, which Watson said he borrowed from his girlfriend. Because Watson was not in actual possession of any of the contraband, the state was obliged to prove constructive possession.

Thus, the state had to establish, beyond a reasonable doubt, that Watson knew of the presence of the illegal items and was able to exercise dominion and control over them.

However, because the car was jointly occupied, Watson's knowledge or control could not be inferred by his mere presence in the car.

Here, the State also had to establish, beyond a reasonable doubt, that Ackon knew of the presence of the ammunition and could maintain control over it.

And because he shared his home with his girlfriend, Ackon's knowledge or control could not be inferred by his mere presence in the home.

The Second said that the state had to prove Watson's knowledge and control by independent proof. The court concluded that the state had not introduced any evidence to prove that Watson had constructive possession of the items found in the trunk.

Furthermore, even though Watson could have seen the handgun from where he was sitting in the driver's seat, this was not enough to prove constructive possession.

The Second wrote, "Even if the state's evidence was sufficient to prove that Watson knew about the gun, it offered no evidence to prove the control element other than Watson's mere proximity to it."

The appellate court emphasized that the state failed to present the required independent proof that Watson had control over the firearm to make a prima facie case of possession of a firearm through constructive possession.

As to the ammunition found in the glove box, the state failed to prove either that Watson knew of its presence or had any control over it. Here, the State's failure to present any independent proof that Ackon knew of the presence of the ammunition or had any ability to maintain control over it was a much greater lack of evidence than found in Watson.

In Watson, the gun was found under the front passenger seat arguably within Watson's reach. The ammunition was found in the glove box.

In our case, who knows where the ammunition was found?

Certainly, there was no evidence that it was found in the same close proximity as the items in Watson. In Coley, a shotgun was found under Coley and his girlfriend's bed.

Coley was charged with possession of a firearm by a convicted felon, but the third concluded that the state failed to prove constructive possession. The appellate court found that the apartment, bedroom, and bed were under the joint control of Coley and his girlfriend.

Therefore, Coley did not have exclusive possession, nor could it be inferred that he could maintain control over the area where the shotgun was found.

Neither may the elements of knowledge and ability to maintain control be inferred in the case below when it was undisputed that Ackon did not have exclusive possession of the house.

If there was evidence as to exactly where the ammunition was found, the State might have been able to establish one or both of those elements. But there was no evidence about where the ammunition was discovered.

As this Court has repeatedly written, a motion for judgment of acquittal should be granted in a case of constructive possession where the evidence is solely circumstantial, and the State fails to present evidence from which the jury can exclude every reasonable hypothesis except that of guilt.

If ever there was a case of circumstantial evidence that failed to exclude every reasonable hypothesis of innocence, this is it. The State's "case" of possession of ammunition by a convicted felon was made up of nothing but innuendo and misrepresentations of law. The prosecutor made some seriously inappropriate remarks in both his first argument and in rebuttal. He argued facts not in evidence (that the ammunition was found near the cannabis).

He told the jury he had to have a good faith basis to bring charges against Ackon, an argument that has repeatedly been held improper.

He argued misstatements of the law (when arguing that the jury could infer that Ackon had knowledge of the ammunition because he admitted he knew about the cannabis).

Some of the prosecutor's improper remarks were objected to; most were not. However, Ackon suggests that the cumulative effect of these highly improper, prejudicial statements was a fundamental error.

The lack of an objection does not bar review on appeal because the comments here amounted to fundamental error. The fundamental error in closing arguments occurs when the prejudicial conduct in its collective import is so extensive that its influence pervades the trial, gravely impairing a calm and dispassionate consideration of the evidence and the merits by the jury.

This Court has held that multiple improprieties in a prosecutor's closing argument may reach "the critical mass of fundamental error" which destroys "the defendant's most important right under our system, the right to the 'essential fairness of (his) criminal trial." In the instant case, the prosecutor engaged in improper and prejudicial closing argument by:

- Improperly making a "good faith" argument;

- Misstating the facts to the jury and arguing facts not in evidence; and

- Misstating the law to the jury. Here, the comments of the prosecutor in his closing argument amounted to fundamental error, warranting a new trial. Improper "Good Faith".

Argument Perhaps the most prejudicial prosecutorial misconduct was when the prosecutor was allowed to make "good faith"

arguments to the jury under the guise of "fair reply."

The prosecution told the jury: "Again, I'll let you be the judge of whose being overzealous and who's jumping around the courtroom. Okay? If I have the opportunity to make an invited response, the allegation is that I'm acting overzealous.

When I file that information, I swear an oath that I can file these charges in good faith. And that's how I proceed. There is no kangaroo court here. There's no conspiracy to get Mr.

Ackon." Unfortunately, the 'curative' instruction (suggested by the State and adopted by the trial court) only made it worse. As in Freeman, the 'curative' instruction only served to emphasize and validate the State's improper comment. An argument that the state only charges those who are guilty is improper.

Appellate courts have condemned such comments as violations of the defendant's right to the presumption of innocence, and compared such comments to telling the jury, 'If the defendant wasn't guilty, he wouldn't be here.'

The prosecutor argued that his 'good faith' comments were justified as a 'fair reply' to the defense's argument that the police and prosecution had acted overzealously.

Defense counsel then modified his argument, after the State's objection, down to saying that the officers 'jumped to conclusions' in this case. It is difficult to understand why the trial court even though defense counsel's closing arguments were improper - or even if it did think it was improper, judging from the transcript. Apparently, the trial court must have agreed with the State (once again) because the court allowed the State to make the improper argument. Anyway, even if Ackon's argument was an improper closing argument, the State went far beyond the limits of propriety when it argued good faith.

Here, Ackon never argued that the State brought the charges in bad faith. The prosecutor's argument below that the State had to have a good-faith basis to prosecute. Ackon was totally improper and highly prejudicial. A misrepresentation of facts not supported by evidence occurred.

The prosecutor told the jury:

"My suggestion would be that his claiming control of this allows you to infer circumstantially that he also had control of this and this and this, certainly if it's found in the same room where he's doing some sort of work with playing games and "as to the unlawful possession of the ammunition, again, this is in the room with the cannabis."

But there was no testimony that the ammunition was found in the same room as the cannabis, the digital scale, or the rolling papers. That was the State's whole problem in attempting to prove this count, as discussed in Point One.

This misstatement was especially critical when considered in light of point one, above, the lack of evidence to support constructive possession of the ammunition. This type of argument did nothing but mask the State's failure to prove the elements of constructive possession.

Closing arguments that are unsupported by the record are improper. The prosecutor overstepped the bounds of the closing argument when he alluded to facts, not in evidence. This, plus the other improper arguments made by the prosecutor, is grounds for reversal.

Misstatements of the Law Finally, the prosecutor improperly told the jury that it could find the "knowledge' and control' elements necessary to prove constructive possession by the fact that Ackon admitted that police would find a small amount of cannabis in the house."

The prosecutor argued:

"We have several kinds of bullets in here... How do we know that it's also in his care, custody, control? Because of the cannabis; when we're talking about the cannabis.

Mr. Ackon said all you're going to find, all you're going to find is the cannabis. So he acknowledged that there's cannabis present. Now you are permitted circumstantially to well, it's a lot like connecting the dots here and there's a hundred dots and the State has gotten up to ninety- eight, you all can step back and look at the picture.

I don't need to put in ninety-nine and one hundred for you all to know what it is. He said all you're going to find is cannabis. Okay? Certainly, admitting to having that would have different consequences than just having this.

My suggestion would be that his claiming control of this allows you to infer circumstantially that he also had control of this and this and this, certainly if it's found in the same room where he's doing some sort of work with playing games."

"[Ackon] says that's my cannabis. Your - it's allowable for you to to circumstantially infer that if he's claiming responsibility for this, all the other contraband that's in that area within his care, custody, control is also in his care, custody, and control even though there's no verbal admission concerning that.

That's perfectly allowable under the law. And I ask you to consider that theory."

"Well, okay, they did find cannabis. But those words [Ackon's admission about the pot) are important because, according to the law, when somebody - if you don't have direct evidence of control or knowledge of contraband and here - well, and here we have this ammunition - both the target- shooting type and the hollow point which is meant to stay in the body and do damage mixed into different kinds of ammo mixed in - as you can see, they're different. You have the copper-jacketed ones meant to stay together and penetrate better. The lead point is meant to expand as it enters the body. It's not permissible to have these under certain circumstances.

Now how do we know that the defendant knew about it? Because there are different kinds of ammo in the box, he said he knew about the cannabis. That's direct evidence of his knowledge.

One of the ways we can tell what people are thinking is if they know about something that's under their control.

"You can assume - it's safe to infer - that he knows about this too." These arguments are a misstatement of the law of constructive possession (or any kind of possession).

The applicable law of possession of ammunition was set out in point one, supra. The prosecutor told the jury that it was 'direct evidence of [Ackon's] knowledge' (of the ammunition) because he knew about the cannabis.

That is not a correct statement of the law. Since the prosecutor repeatedly told the jury this was how they could supply the missing elements of knowledge and control, the jury before must have believed it was proper to do this. Nor can it be said that the error was harmless in this case.

To establish that the error committed at trial was harmless, the state must show 'beyond a reasonable doubt that the error complained of did not contribute to the verdict or, alternatively stated, that there is no reasonable possibility that the error contributed to the conviction.'

At the bar, the cumulative effect of the prosecutor's improper closing argument affected the validity of the trial and, thus, rose to the level of fundamental error requiring a reversal.

Ackon was entitled to a verdict by the jury based solely on the evidence presented at trial.

This was everything in a nutshell.

All I could do from here is pray over this. The state has a chance to respond, and then the courts decide.

13
The Struggle

One thing I loved to do was read. I was walking the yard with a friend named Kenny, and he used to put me onto a lot of self-help books and pro-black novels. He introduced me to a book by George Jackson called "Soledad Brother." George Jackson was an author who wrote prison letters to his lawyer and other female comrades and friends (including Angela Davis). Despite being sentenced for robbery, his letters contained inspiring quotes. One that resonated with me was, "I have developed as a result of living under a ruthless system, a set of mannerisms that numbs the soul. I have been made the floormat of the world, but the world has yet to see what can be done by men of our nature, by men who have walked the path of disparity, of regression, of abortion and yet come out whole. There will be a special page in the book of life for the men who have crawled back from the grave. This page will tell of utter defeat, ruin, passivity and subjection in one breath, and in the next, overwhelming victory and fulfillment." It made so much sense to me. Imagine fighting your whole life for something just to die in the end, and then end up in hell? I waited until the next yard call to ask Kenny his opinion, but they made us all lockdown. When the lockdown was over, I found out Kenny got stabbed and was trauma-hawked to a hospital in Lake Butler. I never heard from him again. He told me that his grandfather once said, "Till remaining the same hurts more than change, you will remain the same." That quote stuck with me to this day. I took the opportunity to help others while I waited for the state to respond or make a decision. I became so good at researching cases that I began helping others with cases like mine. However, the only cases I couldn't fight were violation of probation cases. It didn't matter if you were dead to rights and had merit for violating. It always boiled down to the fact that you "came in contact with law enforcement," making you guilty. If you're on probation, you cannot have any contact with law enforcement, so helping people fight these cases was a waste of time.

There was one guy named Mark who had a case similar to mine, and I spent days working with him on his case. However, he still had an adolescent mentality. One day, we went to the regular yard, and I put my radio down to play basketball, and he stole my radio. That was it; I never spoke to him again. My dorm was called "A" dorm, an open bay consisting of 65 beds per door, and there were five dorms. My bunk sat directly across from the Legal Mail window. I used to pray so hard that my appeal would get granted, and that window was where the answer was coming from. I did everything with that window — ate with it, conversed, laughed, cried. We became best friends. I used to keep my headphones on, and there was a lady named Delilah who used to come on and play uplifting songs and say uplifting quotes. While everyone else was playing hip-hop and rock stations, I always listened to her. There was this song from back in the day by Steve Win wood called "Back in the Highlife Again." I'm a music connoisseur, and I know almost every 80's song, yet I hadn't heard this one until I got a radio in prison. I constantly heard it on the radio, but one moment as I lay in my bunk staring at the Legal Mail window, listening to this song, it became clearer. The song said, "You'll be back in the highlife again, all the doors that were closed one time will open up again." Was that God trying to tell me I would be free one day? Will all the opportunities I had once before, be available again?

In the morning, I did outside grounds for my job assignment. I used to sweep by the Legal Mail window on purpose just to be close to it. The entrance/exit of the prison was behind me and always visible. You could see the double barb-wired fence and the prison employee's vehicles in the parking lot. The average person would think and look to those gates for freedom, but as for me, my back was always turned to those fences, keeping my eye on the Legal Mail window. I just felt like God was showing me that the exit was this way, not behind me. I looked at it as if I was in a dark building and God was trying to show me where the exit was at, but I saw a light in the opposite direction, and I'm telling God this is the exit where the light is at. God's like no, the exit is the opposite way. Now I take matters into my own hands and follow that light, and when I get there, it is just a window.

Father's Day was really bad for me. I haven't even spoken to my kids. My boy Clutch wrote me and said he ran into my kids' mother and her boyfriend. At this point, they'd been dating for almost 2 years.

I found out later that he was a druggie and used to make my kids pick up cigarette butts off the ground for punishment. I trained myself not to think of that because I would've gone crazy in here. Clutch said he approached them and asked to take pictures of the kids for me. The boyfriend got mad, so she took off. That hurt when I read that. On this particular day, I was walking the yard and listening to Orlando's hip-hop station, and the rapper Plies came on the radio and said, "To all those walking in the yard in prison right now thinking about your kids and going through it, if no one told you Happy Father's Day, I'm saying it. Happy Father's Day." I couldn't hold back the tears. Plies had a brother in a federal prison and had been an advocate for prisoners for the longest. He earned all my respect to this day. He understood.

I took this opportunity to write my dad a letter. It started with a poem, and this is how it went: "Since I've been locked away out of everyone's sight, my family has forgotten me almost overnight, a few friends and family are sick, some have even died, people close to me said they would write, but they all had lied. I guess the old saying is true, out of sight out of mind, because everyone has forgotten me in a short period of time. It doesn't matter how much I write, they never write back, they just don't care, I'm forgotten, and it's a pure and simple fact. They claim they are so busy and I believe them to an extent, but it would only take 15 minutes, and a stamp is only 0.42

cents. Now I let them satisfy themselves with this poor excuse, but me, them, and everyone else knows the pitiful truth. I pray to God to keep my faith and help my strength to grow, but when I look at my face in the mirror, the sadness always shows. When I get out, everyone will be happy and welcome me back home, but I'm all alone in here, and when I get out, I just want everyone to leave me alone. I thought about it hard, and believe me, the decision was tough to make, but all the hurt, promises, and lies I could no longer take, so I will continue to be alone and pretend they never existed, for selfishness, lies, and manipulation is all of what consisted." Needless to say my dad never responded to it.

Sundays I usually go to church in the mornings." Always love church, just not the religious type. I felt like religion was man's attempt to put God in the box. This particular day, I went in and there was this man on the piano, singing "How Great Is Our God" as we were getting seated.

He sang it with such passion and soul; it was like you could feel everything he was saying. You could literally see his pain. It was this moment again seriously wanting to advocate for inmates. I just wanted to help. I opened my Bible, and we began reading

Lamentations 3:

"I am the one who has seen the afflictions that come from the rod of the Lord's anger.

He has led me into darkness, shutting out all light. He has turned his hand against me again and again, all day long. He has made my skin and flesh grow old. He has broken my bones.

He has besieged and surrounded me with anguish and distress. He has buried me in a dark place, like those long dead.

He has walled me in, and I cannot escape. He has bound me in heavy chains. And though I cry and shout, he has shut out my prayers.

He has blocked my way with a high stone wall; he has made my road crooked. He has hidden like a bear or a lion, waiting to attack me. He has dragged me off the path and torn me in pieces, leaving me helpless and devastated.

He has drawn his bow and made me the target for his arrows. He shot his arrows deep into my heart. My own people laugh at me. All day long they sing their mocking songs.

He has filled me with bitterness and given me a bitter cup of sorrow to drink. He has made me chew on gravel. He has rolled me in the dust. Peace has been stripped away, and I have forgotten what prosperity is. I cry out, 'My splendor is gone!

Everything I had hoped for from the Lord is lost!' The thought of my suffering and homelessness is bitter beyond words. I will never forget this awful time; I grieve over my loss."

Every single verse was directed towards me; I felt it in my spirit. Then it went on to say:

"Yet I still dare to hope when I remember this. The faithful love of the Lord never ends! His mercies never cease. Great is his faithfulness; his mercies begin afresh each morning. I say to myself, 'The Lord is my inheritance; therefore, I will hope in him!' The Lord is good to those who depend on him, to those who search for him. So it is good to wait quietly for salvation from the Lord. And it is good for people to submit at an early age to the yoke of his discipline: Let them sit alone in silence beneath the Lord's demands. Let them lie face down in the dust, for there may be hope at last. Let them turn the other cheek to those who strike them and accept the insults of their enemies. For no one is abandoned by the Lord forever. Though he brings grief, he also shows compassion because of the greatness of his unfailing love. He does not derive pleasure from causing harm or inflicting sorrow upon others."

I'm thinking to myself wait: verse 31 says no one is abandoned by the Lord forever. I am thinking but God look at my circumstances. I'm sitting in prison for 15 years over a box of bullets. I have not killed anyone. There are people in here with eight life sentences able to call home to family. Everyone abandoned me. I used to envy those people with friends and family. So I decided to write another letter to my dad. In the letter, I just told him that I loved him and not to feel sorry for me. I had to take this trip by myself. As long as when I stand before my God knowing I have done the best I could and have fought the good fight, and God says 'Well done my faithful servant' as he welcomes me in Paradise. You know Dad; I'm not going to make those excuses like I did not ask to be brought into this world. I am in prison for something that I did not do. Right, you can sleep in the presence of serial killers and rapists and extortionist, etc., you name them. I sleep with one eye open and my shoes on every night. It is a whole different world in here and I can't begin to explain. What I admire is that the same people with twelve life sentences and 450 years to run concurrently are the same ones I consider the most fortunate because they still have families and friends that ride with them, they can call home, people send those letters, money and they live all right. No one cared I got 15 years. Personally, I don't believe anyone believes that I was innocent, no one cares. I respect everyone's decision. I will continue to spend every breathing minute of my life fighting this case to be with my two children. I do not need sympathy. When I do come home just please do not play the role of the father to the prodigal son. This goes for everyone. God does not abandon anyone forever; he is too merciful! Rest in peace to Uncle Kofi and their family members that passed and I knew nothing about. I still don't know if he got that letter.

I picked up a new routine of working out and running to release some stress and anxiety. It has been months, and nothing has come back yet on my appeal. The anxiety is killing me but I'm still trusting.

On this particular day, I was running back to my dorm, and I arrived next to my bunk sweating. There was a random honey bun on my bunk.

I instantly remember the story of what would happen if I ate it. It was as if a bubble Caption popped over my head with my boy city in it saying, 'Don't eat it!' Then the bubble popped.

I think it's me that I'm only in year one. I have about 14 more to go and if I'm going to get raped let me handle the situation now I don't care if I live or die. So I waited till count time was done.

There is a little gap where the COs leaves to the next dorm to count others and it's quiet, then it gets noisier. Within that little gap, I jumped up off my bunk and yelled, 'AYO! Someone left a honey bun on my bunk!'

Then I broke it open and said, 'If you want it come get it!' Then I lay in my bunk with a whole bunch of colored pencils sharpened and tied together with strings for the sheets of the bed and waited.

At this point, if a friend would've walked up to ask to borrow a pencil, I would've just started chewing his neck! I was extremely paranoid. About an hour later my crew walked up laughing because they pranked me. My heart dropped. They had to be the cruelest prank in history.

Every time I read the Bible I always kept being referred to that specific story about Joseph. There was something in a story that I wanted you to know. Just didn't know what it was. Read it at least 30 times.

Almost a year and a half in and he struggles by realizing more and more that prison is not for me, or anyone for that matter. The main item I consumed from the commissary list was ramen soup, and its price was doubled. Additionally, I often play Scrabble and have extensively studied the third and fourth editions of the Scrabble dictionary. I played people for commissary.

One day I was playing this with one guy and we were arguing over a word and whether we could put an 'S' behind it. As we argued back-and-forth the argument turned more and more serious.

Then he said something crazy. He said, 'What kind of dumb ass turns down five years probation to get 15 years in prison anyway?' That struck me. It proved that everyone knew about my situation. It brought me back to when I was in my cell block writing letters and people walking by pointing at me and whispering like I was a laughingstock. Back when I was in jail there was a guy by the name of Eric that turned down 15 months' probation and got seven years when he lost trial.

I remember everybody talking about him and it was like he was the butt of everybody's jokes. I even made fun of him. I actually beat him out with my situation. Wow. It made me pray even harder than my appeal goes through.

It was difficult for me to find weed in prison. But when I found it boy! Smoking felt like job corps without the women. But be prepared for drug testing. They call random names every day so you had to stay 'juiced up,' in other words, stay hydrated with plenty of water.

We always walked around with cups of water as if we were drinking liquor on the streets. If they take you in for the test and you feel it's automatically 60 days in the box with all your gained time you have achieved gone.

So if you had done 10 years already and earned 3 years worth of gain time they will take those 3 years. I didn't care I still smoked. It was too stressful in there. At least we had sports, but even then when the time hits 10 o'clock we all have to go in for count and then bed. We never get to finish games.

So if you have bets you find out by radio or the next day. Something violent happens at least once a day in that place. It was always a code red where the COs Were running in someone's dorms whether for a fight or stabbing or shakedown, where they searched up belongings.

I always kept him. I said, 'Where I was going to die in here.' So I kept a lock in a sock under my pillow and a shank (homemade knife) in the "Rec" yard. I remember keeping it by the yellow post and it was buried. I would wait till "Rec" then I would dig it up. I had issues with this one guy named Bouie.

And the rumor was he was waiting for me to 'get wrong' and he was going to handle me. My head was always on a swivel.

Bouie Had 46 years so I knew one of these years he would try to make a move.

I was always plotting for a time to get him first. It was all about timing.

I was on the basketball team which made time fly. There was this one guy named Black!! That was the best player on the whole pound 'always dunking'. Shot went in l were like water. I used to like sitting back and watching him play. The man had a hole in his trachea that healed up. Time went by when I was walking the yard with City and he asked me if I knew what Black was in for.

I was curious now but never thought to ask. He said Black was from Orlando and he was a jack boy (armed robber). There was a young man whose dad was the contractor for kilos and blacks used to always rob him.

In fact, he robbed that guy nine separate times! I always thought someone would learn by the fifth time. Well on the 10th time, the man was at a car wash when he saw Black pull up. I guess Black got comfortable to the point he let his guard down.

Whatever the case, this time this young man was ready, Black stepped out of the car to run towards him. The young man shot Black seven times as he was leaving in his car. The last shot hit Black in the throat.

Black survived and went to court to testify on the man who shot him. The man ended up getting 44 years in prison. I felt like I could not respect that.

Now every time Black played, and the crowd would cheer as he made a basket, I would sit back with a disgusted look on my face, but that all comes with the game.

There was this old man who slept across from me who had been down since the early 60s from camp to camp. He had Canteen items that no longer existed. Pajamas with a hat that had a furry ball on the top, even his chess pieces were tall people-like figures.

I asked him about his items, and he took it as I was trying to be funny. We almost fought over it. I could not put my hands on an old man like that, so I just ignored him and put my headphones on. As I turned on the station Delilah was on, and she kept telling me to wait on God as she continued to play soothing music.

Staring at the Legal Mail window just brought tears to my eyes.

The chances of an appeal to be granted were slim to none. Should I just begin the post-conviction relief process? But if I do then that means I don't believe God can come through for me.

I have no one on the streets except my boy clutch. God used to speak to me through the legal mail window. God had to get me alone.

There are certain situations where God will not allow anyone to help you, and he breaks you down to your lowest common denominator to build you back up. Even a seed must die when it's put into the ground before it springs forth life.

Then I asked God why was I going through all this? Then I opened my bible and it fell on Isaiah 41.

The 10th verse said, "Fear not for I am with you, be not dismayed for I am your God. I will help you. I will strengthen you. I will uphold you with my victorious right hand." I trust you God but the wait is killing me.

Then I looked up and right above that chapter was the one before (Isaiah 40:27-31) and it said, "Oh Israel, how can you say the Lord does not see your troubles? How can you say God refuses to hear your case? Have you never heard or understood? Don't you know that the Lord is the everlasting God, the creator of all the earth? He never grows faint or weary. No one can measure the depths of his understanding. He gives power to those who are tired and worn out; he offers strength to the weak. Even the youths will become exhausted and young man will give up, but those who wait on the lord will find new strength. They will fly high on wings like eagles.

They will run and not grow weary. They will walk and not faint."

A few days later I was getting a drink of water from the water fountain and a man walked up to me and said he was in prayer.

He continued to say, "God told me to tell you, if you can come out of this world, He can make you a great man." Then he walked off. I did not understand.

However, I did dwell on it. Even so, often I would switch Bunkie because a lot of them would either go to the box or get transferred. This particular Bunkie I had was a weird guy, a Muslim but I actually saw him stab someone and come back to the dorm and lie like nothing even happened.

Every month the COs would hand us a gain time sheet and on that gain time sheet it gives you 10 days of credit for good behavior, and it also shows your tentative release date on the bottom of the page. In this particular situation, the officer mixed the paperwork up and gave me my Bunkie paperwork and gave him mine by accident. I looked at it and when I saw the release date, I instinctively yelled a profane word that got everyone in the dorm's attention.

The CEO said oh wait, my mistake, and grabbed our paperwork, and switched it back. My Bunky laughed, I was still in shock. When the correction officer left, people approached me to ask what I saw. I never told anyone. Whatever it was I saw just made me want to hit the law library even harder and pray. That guy is never coming home.

I had a friend named Bertila that really held me down with the letters. It was the only thing I had to look forward to. She was such a good friend to me. When I met her, I used to live in my friend Sanjay's basement in Carteret, New Jersey.

The first time she came to my house, I had other friends who also came over, and she checked them all and made them take their shoes off, and they showed respect to my small room.

She was like a feisty Pitbull. Since then I knew she was going to be my best friend for life. I was very vulnerable there and I always thought when I came home, I was going to marry her. But she was too much of a friend to me. It would never have worked.

Jadakiss from a rap group called D-Block, had a line in one of his songs that went, "I know people go to jail just to get their teeth fixed." That could not be truer because in the penal system at that time around 2008-2009, it only cost four dollars to fix your teeth, anything wrong with it.

The only problem there is a waiting list so in April they finally called my name for Dental. I've been there like a year and a half already I was so excited to go down there to get my teeth fixed I was skipping and COs from the towers were like, "No running!" I was like, "OK, I apologize."

I get to the dentist they look at my mouth and say, "OK. We know what needs to be done. We will schedule your next visit 3 years from now to 2012." I was like that is 3 years from now! "You got to be kidding me."

So mind you, I am livid at this point walking back, the canteen line was open and I was so angry I didn't even see the line that was there already. All I saw was a canteen store right in front of me when I walked back into the open bay dorm.

I slammed my card down ferociously on the counter and said I wanted the 18-wheeler which is a 6ft sub. Also, six honey buns and 12 bags of chips.

The guy in front of the line to my right goes, "Oh, so you do not see somebody standing here, you are just going to go ahead and just walk right up and order?"

I was just so angry at the time I said, "What? Fuck that, do something." He says, "Ok, when we get back in the dorm put your sneakers on and tighten me up (which means fight)."

I still was not paying attention to him. I had a net bag full of food and went back into my dorm. I slept on the top bunk, so I put all my stuff in my locker hopped on my bunk, and started reading a rap magazine.

About 10 minutes later he walked in threw his bags by his bunk and yelled across the room, "Get there." This was how mad I was, I did not even remember it happening, I had the sheets halfway on my body relaxing! I saw him coming towards me, so I just had to get up.

Now, mind you, there are a whole bunch of beds in the middle of the floor and they are all metal. There's really no room to scrap so we both have our fists in the air. I said, "Let's go in the shower." He goes, "No, fuck that, and let's do it here." I said, "OK."

So I swung because I thought I had an opening he weaved it up and caught me with such precision that the temple and eye connected.

All I saw was a light flash.

I went down and as I fell I saw this blue light and a vision of that same guy hitting a baseball. The vision was funny because we were still in prison.

We were just outside in the yard and he hit a home run and he was running on all the bases tapping each one as he ran around the field. Everybody was cheering for him as he was waving to everybody. As I was watching him all of a sudden, it was like the light zoomed back into reality and I was lying on the floor and I saw him standing over me ready to punch me again, but he did not.

Right then it hit me. Oh yeah. This was the Iron Man of the pound. This was a guy who played every sport and excelled at every sport in the whole prison. He played basketball, baseball, soccer, he even ran track and all the games in between and he beat everyone at them. I picked the right one to challenge. I was taking one step forward and two steps back. I kept getting into trouble because I was stressing.

14

His right arm

Back at my dorm, I grabbed some canteen and began making ramen soup, The intercom comes on, and they say on the intercom, "The following inmate's line up for legal mail window after chow." They called 4 names, and one of those 4 was mine, Bernard Ackon. I fell silent. I thought, but this could be anything. The appellate courts asking for me to send more researched case laws, but it's been over a year and a half. This could be the results I've been waiting for.

I went to eat, but to be honest, I couldn't eat. I couldn't even pray.

All I kept reciting in my head was scriptures. Especially Joshua 1:9, "Have not I commanded thee? Be strong and of good courage; be not afraid, neither be thou dismayed: for the LORD thy God is with thee whithersoever thou goest."

I went to the chow hall to eat but ended up giving my tray away. I knocked on the table, got up, and went to line up at the legal man window.

The line took forever. All I did was staring at the building. I couldn't even pray. For the first time in my life, I had no words. All I remember was Luke 1:37, "With God all things are possible." Genesis 18:14, "Is anything too hard for the Lord?" Jeremiah 32:17, "Ah Lord God, thou hast made the heaven and earth by thy great power and outstretched arm; nothing is too difficult for thee." Isaiah 50:2, "Is my hand shortened at all that it cannot redeem?" I genuinely felt like God was talking to me.

The mail lady looked at my ID tag to confirm it was me and handed me an envelope. I then walked back to my dorm. My boy City X asked me, "Is that the letter?"

I told him not to talk to me right now because this moment was the moment where I win or I break. It was similar to the verdict when I went through the second trial and my lawyer tried to put his arms around me, and I pushed it off.

No one could join me at this moment because it was just me and God. I went to my bunk, sat down, and just looked at the sky. All I said was, "Not my will be done, but yours." I opened the letter. It said:

Congratulations, your case has been reversed.

I just sat with absolutely no emotion.

The appellate judge's opinion:

The defendant appeals his convictions and sentences for assault on a law enforcement officer, possession of ammunition by a convicted felon, possession of cannabis, and use or possession of drug paraphernalia. He first argues the trial court erred in denying his motion for judgment of acquittal as it related to the possession of ammunition by a convicted felon.

We agree and reverse the conviction and sentence on that count only. We affirm the convictions and sentences on the remaining counts.

Law enforcement received information that the defendant was selling crack cocaine and set up a controlled buy. On the day of the transaction, the police observed the defendant leaving his driveway with his girlfriend in his girlfriend's car.

A trash pulls from the defendant's residence revealed marijuana, which law enforcement used to establish probable cause for a search warrant. When the officers executed the search warrant, they knocked and entered the residence.

In one unoccupied room, they found a video game on pause. As they opened the door to the garage, a dog attempted to charge into the home.

One of the detectives went outside and found that the garage door had been opened and saw the defendant walking out of the garage. At that point, the dog attacked the detective giving rise to the assault charge.

Another detective detained the defendant, and read him the search warrant and Miranda warnings. As the officers began to conduct the search, the defendant told them they were not going to find anything other than a small amount of marijuana belonging to him. Testimony revealed that several officers searched the house, while a single detective remained in the dining room and documented the items found: ammunition, a digital scale, less than twenty grams of cannabis, and some cigarette rolling papers.

The detective who actually found the ammunition did not testify and no one was able to testify where the ammunition had been found. One of the detectives explained that there may have been officers who approached from the back of the house to ensure that no one left through the back door.

A firearms examiner from the crime lab testified that there were three different types of ammunition inside the box. Over defense objection, the examiner was allowed to testify concerning the types of ammunition, the typical use of each bullet *1148* design, and that all the rounds could be fired from the same firearm.

The defendant moved for a judgment of acquittal on the possession of ammunition count, arguing that the State had failed to prove an essential element of the crime: knowledge of the ammunition.

The defendant argued that there had been no proof of where the ammunition had been found or if it had even been found in the house. While pictures had been taken of the items seized, the ammunition was not in the photos.

The State responded that the defendant's admission concerning the cannabis established that he had knowledge of the ammunition, which had been found in the same room.

However, significantly, no one had testified that the ammunition had been found in the same room. The State then offered to postpone the trial so that it could call another officer.

The trial judge responded that the search took place in the home and the ammunition had been found there with the defendant being the only occupant.

The defendant argued, however, that the warrant actually indicated that there were two residents of the house. The trial court denied the motion.

In closing, the State argued that the box of mixed ammunition established that someone had had it because it didn't come packaged that way.

In addition, the defendant's admission to the cannabis further established that the defendant had the care, custody, and control of the ammunition.

The State asked the jury to use its common sense in considering whether the defendant's girlfriend could have owned the ammunition and reminded the jury that there could be joint possession.

The jury failed to reach a verdict on the counts of possession of cocaine and sale or delivery of cocaine but found the defendant guilty of assault on a law enforcement officer, possession of ammunition, cannabis, and drug paraphernalia.

The defendant was later found not guilty of possession and sale of cocaine. The trial court sentenced the defendant to fifteen years for the possession of ammunition count.

On appeal, the defendant argues that the State failed in its burden of proof because no one testified to the location of the ammunition and the house was occupied (although not at the time of the warrant's execution) by more than one person.

The State responded that the defendant's admission to possession of marijuana within the house and the mixed ammunition in the box was sufficient to prove beyond a reasonable doubt that the defendant possessed the ammunition. We disagree with the State. We review the trial court's ruling on the motion for judgment of acquittal de novo (Beckford v. State, 964 So. 2d 793, 795 (Fla. 4th DCA 2007)).

In moving for a judgment of acquittal, the defendant "admits the facts adduced in evidence and every conclusion favorable to the state which is fairly and reasonably inferable there from" (Maglio v. State, 918 So. 2d 369, 374 (Fla. 4th DCA 2005)).

A motion for judgment of acquittal should not be granted "unless the evidence is such that no view which the jury may lawfully take of it favorable to the opposite party can be sustained under the law" (Darling v. State, 808 So. 2d 145, 155 (Fla.2002) (quoting Lynch v. State, 293 So. 2d 44, 45 (Fla. 1974)).

The State charged the defendant with possession of ammunition by a convicted felon, according to section 790.23(1), Florida Statutes (2007). The State advanced the theory of constructive, and not actual, possession.

This required the State to prove the defendant: a) knew the contraband was in his presence;

b) Could maintain control over it; and

c) Knew of the illicit nature of the contraband (Williams v. State,724 So. 2d 1214, 1215 (Fla. 4th DCA 1998)).

When the area in which the contraband is found is within the defendant's exclusive possession, his guilty knowledge of the presence of the contraband and his ability to maintain control over it may be inferred.

However, "if the property where the contraband found is in joint rather than exclusive possession of the accused, then knowledge of the contraband's presence and the ability to control it will not be inferred from the accuser's presence but must be established by independent proof " (Id.).

Here, there was no direct testimony that the ammunition was even found in the house. Without this testimony, the State could not meet its burden of establishing beyond a reasonable doubt that the defendant knew the ammunition was in his presence or that he could maintain control over it (Id.).

We therefore reverse the defendant's conviction on the count alone and remand the case to the trial court to vacate the judgment and sentence on that count. Reversed and Remanded.

I fell to my knees and spoke with my eyes open.

I don't remember exactly what I prayed, but I remember saying, "Since the world began, no ear has heard and no eye has seen a God like you, who works for those who wait on Him. I couldn't Thank you enough Lord."

One month later, on July 15, 2009, I had just finished Bible study with a few of my peers. We were discussing prosperity preachers and how it was wrong for them to have jet planes and million-dollar houses.

Their argument to me was how in scripture it says in Luke 10:7

"...For the laborer is worthy of his hire."

It made sense, but I felt like it wasn't justification for the private jets and hustling the churches.

As I'm talking, my name gets called; "Bernard Ackon report of classification." The only time your name gets called to classification is when they are changing your job or you are moving to another door.

So I make my way downstairs and go into one of the personnel's offices. I noticed she was on a landline phone. She says a few words to finish her convoy and hangs up.

The lady asked me my name, checked my ID and told me, "Well, Mr. Ackon, it looks as if your case has been overturned. You don't qualify for the hundred dollars you get upon release. You don't qualify for a one-way ticket anywhere United States by bus. We just have to release you.

So, I need you to sign here, here, and here." I looked at the paper, and the paper I was signing said, I was going to be on CRD

(conditional release), curfew for 24 hours, report to someone, etc. I said, "I am sorry, ma'am, I can't sign that. I came here an innocent

man I will leave here an innocent man."

She looked at me with a shocked face. The only other look I remember similar was the bailiff who walked me downstairs after I turned down five years of probation.

The lady said, "Hold on a second." She picked up the phone and called the head secretary of the Department of Corrections and asked, "How do we do a vacated sentence? We have never done one before."

I could hear him through the landline phone she was on, and he said, "He just signs a piece of paper saying he is released, and he has to be released immediately because if anything happens to him

from here, it is considered a lawsuit in the penal system."

She says, "okay," and hangs up the phone. I immediately said, "I heard." So she scribbled out everything that pertains to CRD and handed the paper to me to sign at the bottom. But I knew how they played.

I asked for her initials everywhere she scribbled out. She laughed and put her initials on everywhere she scribbled. They went upstairs and packed my belongings because I could not go back upstairs.

I went through a process where I had to go through a whole checkout. A man was sitting in medical, and it was just me and him in the room. My whole being was still in a state of shock. It still hadn't hit me.

The guy in the room asked me if I was going home. I spoke, "This moment had to happen. As shocking as these sounds I cannot die right now because God had this moment planned already. When God says it is time, it is time!! No devil in hell can stop this moment."

They gave me some donated clothes and sneakers (ironically a pair of Jordans). And two police officers escorted me out. They put me in a van and took me to the nearest bus station in

Ocala, Florida. They dropped me off and left. I told the cashier at the bus terminal what happened to me and she felt bad and bought me a ticket back to St. Lucie County.

On that bus ride back I couldn't help but to reflect. It seems so surreal. I held strong to my faith believing that God was not going to fail when I needed him the most.

Deep within, I knew but outwardly I had doubt that it's a reality that no one wins appeals and everyone knows this. So, I was in there dealing with constant doubt from others and doubt from myself. But I stood strong in my belief.

Throughout the whole Bible, the one word that stuck out to me was "waiting." "The eyes of the Lord run to and fro the whole earth showing himself strong on behalf of the ones whose heart are perfect towards him" (2 Chronicles 16:9).

I was far from perfect but my heart was and always had love for Him. I turned what was supposed to be an institution into a university.

Defied the odds, I arrived at a bus station in Fort Pierce Florida. The only things I had on my hands were books and paperwork, which were tied up in one huge pillow bag. Feels like I've been gone forever but it has only been two years.

I remember my friend Will's number by heart. He had the same number for at least 20 years. I called, and he answered; he thought he heard a ghost. He asked where I was, and he would pick me up immediately so he came. He took me to Clutch's house it was so good to see my brother.

I fell asleep in his room. I woke up the next morning to his mom (which I consider my mom) Diving on top of me and praising God and praying. I ended up living there for a while.

Word eventually got around that I was home. Nobody could believe it. They thought I was gone forever. My family was trying to get a hold of me. People in the streets thought I was a snitch wondering how I get out of that situation.

I really didn't care what people thought at that time. I finally went to my kids' school to see them. It was tears of joy.

They were so happy to see me. I spent the next few months trying to figure out ways to sue because of the time I lost but no one wanted to take up my case.

The ones that even wanted to hear about it even said I couldn't win because I was guilty of the misdemeanors so there's a stipulation and I couldn't sue.

I gave up on that. I got a job working as a dishwasher making $10 an hour trying to get back adapted in this life. I was getting up from the table after eating I knocked on the table as if I was still in prison. I was so institutionalized. I even wrote my DC number on envelopes when I sent mail. After a while, my old girlfriend became cool to the point we could actually speak to each other. I guess the saying is true time really does heal things.

At this time me and my girlfriend actually got married and just had another baby. I remember God telling me to tell everyone what he did for me but just like the story of Jonah, I didn't.

I just went about figuring life out I eventually had to leave the one house I was living at because the house has been closed.

So, I called on my kids' mother to help me move my stuff out. She lived in a one-bedroom house, and she offered me to come to stay with her and my kids.

The kids were very happy to see the family back together again but living in a one-bedroom house was hard.

They were still in elementary school, and they went to bed at 9 o'clock, so when they went to bed, I went to bed. I struggled to finally save up enough money to get a better house to rent.

I was working at a call center around this time, and I have been home for five years now. I was driving a soccer mom van that barely ran and living paycheck to paycheck.

I have been waiting for months for a check from the IRS to get a working vehicle. It's my surprise the letter finally came. I was so excited I didn't even want to open it, so I got to work.

After a few calls, I opened it up, and the letter said I was a victim of identity theft and it would take over 11 months to clear the situation. I was so depressed I just walked out of work and didn't clock out or anything.

I went home, but as soon as I got there, I opened the door to see my wife holding our new baby with electricity off in the house. My wife asked what we were going to do, and I didn't have any money. I dropped the items from my hands and went to the bathroom, got on my knees, and prayed.

Usually, I pray with my eyes closed. The only other time I prayed this intensely was when I needed God to come through on the appeal when I was in prison and there was no other option.

This was similar, so my eyes were wide open as I prayed. I said, "God, I am 34 years old. I have no skill. My past haunts me, I have a family, I can't even take care of, I don't have credit and I'm in debt. You got me out of prison and told me I would be great.

I feel like you got me out of prison to fail. And God if this is all I have to look forward to, please take me out of here and this life." The tears immediately began to roll down.

A week later, my friend Korey called me and said his friend Danny was doing a moving job for a company and he needed one more guy for the unload.

I did not have work that day, so I agreed, and I could use the money. I had no experience in moving; in fact, I hated moving. Halfway through that job, I and he sat down to eat lunch, and Danny was sitting across from me.

A sand hill crane walked up and just stood there between us. It was so close that it was within arm's reach. I flinched at it to scare it off; however, it didn't move.

I said, "Oh, you want to help us move?" So I got my phone out and took a picture of the sand hill crane. The way I took the picture made it look like the sand hill crane was biting the hand truck we're using for the move.

I pointed it out to Danny, and all he said was cool. For the next few days, I dwell on that picture. My heart was tugging at starting up a moving company.

I reached out to a nonprofit organization group that helps people who try to start up businesses. I went there, and some old man was a volunteer there. Everything I told the man that I wanted to do, I kept getting a negative response.

I told him all my ideas and every answer was "you can't do that". After an hour of his denials, I thanked him for his time and left. I then walked across the street to a pawnshop to look for a hand truck.

At the time I had $50 in my name, a single bill. I asked the guy at the pawnshop how much for one of those hand trucks. He was counting money from the register and said $45.

I then asked if he could do it for $40 so I could have $10 left to eat but I only had $50. He said no very stern. I said okay and bought it, put it into the soccer van.

A few days later, my sister came to visit me and I told her my plan. She walked me through the basis of starting a business, and she asked me what I would like the name of the business to be.

I looked into the sky, and it looked like the intro to a Star Wars movie where the words roll down slanted in space. I saw the word SAFELY, followed by the letter N. Then the word SWIFT followed by MOVERS. Then I saw the sentence, "Quality movers you could rely on..." I looked at my sister and said, "Safely N Swift Movers!"

She was amazed at how fast I came up with the name. She said people take days to come up with names. I told her I had just seen it in the sky.

After that process, I began getting jobs on my own, and for every job I did, a sandhill crane would appear. When we would drive to work I would see one, or within the vicinity, one would pass by.

And every time I knew it was God. I even used the verse from Ecclesiastes 9:10 "Whatsoever you find to do with your hands do with all your might..." In hindsight, I realize that God cut off everything for me to make me focus solely on him.

No one could help me even if they wanted to. The tribulations I was going through were designed for me to give me strength, build up my faith and also my trust, and sense the will of God for my life. All my life I have been known to fight. If you look back on my life you would notice that that's all I ever did. Then when this whole situation happened, it showed a whole different fight.

Every trouble that I went through was the plate that God put on a spiritual iron bar that I was using to work out. The more weight got put on me, the stronger I got. So did my faith.

This situation gave me a chance to know God on a very personal level, and I realized that God is a God of impossibility.

In my experience, I realize that God waits till the situation becomes so impossible that when he gets you out of it, there's no way anyone can say that they did it themselves or they had help. His signature is on the deliverance, and no one else can take credit.

Picture of parade that you are in when you are in the parade, you can only see so far because there are people in front of you and there are people behind you.

There is no way to see the end of the parade. Now if you were above the parade, you could see the whole picture, the beginning, and the end. But if you are above the parade, you have a clear view of the whole parade. God has the whole view. He saw things I didn't because I was "in" the parade.

The legal mail window was God's way of showing me that his ways aren't my ways and my thoughts aren't his. The times I was outside, I could have been more focused on the gates for my freedom.

Instead, I looked towards the legal Mail window for my freedom. Sometimes we see a light in a dark room and we can literally swear that it is the exit. But God can be telling us "On the exit is the dark area which is the opposite way". You ignore God's direction because you see a light. Then when you get there, the whole time that light was just a window that would have been my experience had I not listened.

The reason for building the moving company off Ecclesiastes 9:10 was because it said whatever you find to do with your hands, do it with all your might. I used every breath, every thought, and every ounce of my being to focus on getting out through the law books. All that energy prevailed in the end. It was only right to build a company off of that verse because you only become successful by putting 100% into it.

The story of Joseph was the basis of everything I went through. The storyline was so similar in many ways. In every tribulation that he went through, God was still with him.

He was innocent in everything and succeeded in everything because of that. Noticing in that story he had a dream that he will one day become a prince. Throughout his life, nothing seemed even the slightest as if it would be possible.

His brothers tried to kill him, accused him of rape and he was put in prison for 13 years. Yet God had a reason that Joseph couldn't see because he was "in the parade" and not above it, so he couldn't see the end.

There was a famine coming up where the only place to get food was going to be in Egypt. The only way for the Hebrews to eat was to put a Hebrew person in position in Egypt to be able to feed the Hebrews.

All the trials and tribulations Joseph went through were to condition him for that position. It was everything he went through that built him to know what to do in that situation.

To be a leader

Now that Joseph was in that position he could've chosen to take any kind of vengeance. Instead, he told his brothers, "Not to be angry with themselves because they sold him here God sent him before you to preserve life" (Gen.45:5).

What they meant for evil God used for good. The same way with me, I am in the law books now and people are using the keys to my case and quoting my case to overturn their cases. But I had to go through it just like Joseph did.

Everyone who claimed they loved me left my side, people hated me, and some were glad I was gone. I could have harbored all that hatred instead I used it to help because the blessings were not for me it was for others.

In the book of Exodus Moses ran off to the wilderness and spent 40 years there after killing an Egyptian that was beating a Hebrew slave.

Moses was a Hebrew himself who became an Egyptian citizen after his mom sent him off to Egypt. God eventually called Moses to return to go and get the Hebrew slaves out of Egypt.

This shows two things. One, God will take you out of a terrible situation and then tell you to go back there to get the ones left behind. And second, God always uses one from the pack that he saves to return to get others.

The same Law books I studied now have my own case law in them and people are using my case law "Ackon vs. State" to overturn their cases. I realize now that everything I went through was not for me it was for others.

Now God has brought me back to where he had removed me to show people how they can fight their cases. People get locked up and just go "lie down" knowing that they are innocent.

They will let time fly by and later on realize there was a loophole but then is too late because time expired. I pray that my story will help someone fight because St. Lucie County, the county that I live in, has a judicial system that is so corrupt.

Lawyers and prosecutors are swapping people's lives out depending on who is paying more. People are getting over-sentenced. Look at me! I got 15 years over a box of bullets that no one knew where it came from.

This book's intention is to delve into this weak system of corruption. It is also worth noting that my original name was supposed to be Joseph. My father went behind my mom's back and took me to the Catholic church where they gave me the name

Bernard, named after my grandfather.

My mother was furious when she found out. So the whole time Joseph was me and I was Joseph. And the prosecutor that was in my case when I went to trial was allegedly fired over my case and is now a defense attorney.

14 So.3d 1146 (2009)

Bernard ACKON, Appellant,

v.

STATE of Florida, Appellee.

No. 4D08-970.[1]

District Court of Appeal of Florida, Fourth District.

June 17, 2009.

[1] . https://scholar.google.com/scholar?scidkt=13598096656648292073&as_sdt=2&hl=en

*1147 Carey Haughwout, Public Defender, and Dea Abramschmitt, Assistant Public Defender, West Palm Beach, for appellant.

Bill McCollum, Attorney General, Tallahassee, and Georgina Jimenez-Orosa, Assistant Attorney General, West Palm Beach, for appellee.

MAY, J.

The defendant appeals his convictions and sentences for assault on a law enforcement officer, possession of ammunition by a convicted felon, possession of cannabis, and use or possession of drug paraphernalia. He first argues the trial court erred in denying his motion for judgment of acquittal as it related to the possession of ammunition by a convicted felon. We agree and reverse the conviction and sentence on that count only. We affirm the convictions and sentences on the remaining counts.

Law enforcement received information that the defendant was selling crack cocaine and set up a controlled buy. On the day of the transaction, the police observed the defendant leaving his driveway with his girlfriend in his girlfriend's car. A trash pull from the defendant's residence revealed marijuana, which law enforcement used to establish probable cause for a search warrant.

When the officers executed the search warrant, they knocked and entered the residence. In one unoccupied room, they found a video game on pause. As they opened the door to the garage, a dog attempted to charge into the home. One of the detectives went outside and found that the garage door had been opened and saw the defendant walking out of the garage. At that point, the dog attacked the detective giving rise to the assault charge.

Another detective detained the defendant, and read him the search warrant and *Miranda* warnings. As the officers began to conduct the search, the defendant told them they were not going to find anything other than a small amount of marijuana belonging to him.

Testimony revealed that several officers searched the house, while a single detective remained in the dining room and documented the items found: ammunition, a digital scale, less than twenty grams of cannabis, and some cigarette rolling papers.

The detective who actually found the ammunition did not testify and no one was able to testify where the ammunition had been found. One of the detectives explained that there may have been officers that approached from the back of the house to insure that no one left through the back door.

A firearms examiner from the crime lab testified that there were three different types of ammunition inside the box. Over defense objection, the examiner was allowed to testify concerning the types of ammunition, the typical use of each bullet *1148 design, and that all the rounds could be fired from the same firearm. The defendant moved for a judgment of acquittal on the possession of ammunition count, arguing that the State had failed to prove an essential element of the crime: knowledge of the ammunition. The defendant argued that there had been no proof of where the ammunition had been found or if it had even been found in the house. While pictures had been taken of the items seized, the ammunition was not in the photos.

The State responded that the defendant's admission concerning the cannabis established that he had knowledge of the ammunition, which had been found in the same room. However, significantly no one had testified that the ammunition had been found in the same room. The State then offered to postpone the trial so that it could call another officer. The trial judge responded that the search took place in the home and the ammunition had been found there with the defendant being the only occupant. The defendant argued however that the warrant actually indicated that there were two residents of the house. The trial court denied the motion.

In closing, the State argued that the box of mixed ammunition established that someone had been in possession of it because it didn't come packaged that way. In addition, the defendant's admission to the cannabis further established that the defendant had the care, custody, and control of the ammunition. The State asked the jury to use its common sense in considering whether the defendant's girlfriend could have been in possession of the ammunition and reminded the jury that there could be joint possession.

The jury failed to reach a verdict on the counts for possession of cocaine and sale or delivery of cocaine, but found the defendant guilty of assault on a law enforcement officer, possession of ammunition, cannabis, and drug paraphernalia. The defendant was later found not guilty of possession and sale of cocaine. The trial court sentenced the defendant to fifteen years for the possession of ammunition count.

On appeal, the defendant argues that the State failed in its burden of proof because no one testified to the location of the ammunition and the house was occupied (although not at the time of the warrant's execution) by more than one person. The State responds that the defendant's admission to possession of marijuana within the house and the mixed ammunition in the box was sufficient to prove beyond a reasonable doubt that the defendant possessed the ammunition. We disagree with the State.

We review the trial court's ruling on the motion for judgment of acquittal *de novo*. *Beckford v. State*, 964 So.2d 793, 795 (Fla. 4th DCA 2007)[2]. In moving for a judgment of acquittal, the defendant "admits the facts adduced in evidence and every conclusion favorable to the state which is fairly and reasonably inferable therefrom." *Maglio v. State*, 918 So.2d 369, 374 (Fla.

---

[2] . https://scholar.google.com/
    scholar_case?case=17739472873677078392&q=ackon+v+state&hl=en&as_sdt=80006

4th DCA 2005)[3]. A motion for judgment of acquittal should not be granted "unless the evidence is such that no view which the jury may lawfully take of it favorable to the opposite party can be sustained under the law." _Darling v. State_, 808 So.2d 145, 155 (Fla.2002)[4] (quoting _Lynch v. State_, 293 So.2d 44, 45 (Fla. 1974)[5]).

The State charged the defendant with possession of ammunition by a convicted felon, pursuant to section 790.23(1), Florida Statutes (2007). The State advanced the theory of constructive, and not actual, possession. This required the State to prove the defendant: (1) knew the contraband was in his presence; (2) had *1149 the ability to maintain control over it; and (3) knew of the illicit nature of the contraband. _Williams v. State_, 724 So.2d 1214, 1215 (Fla. 4th DCA 1998)[6].

When "the area in which the contraband is found is within the defendant's _exclusive_ possession, his guilty knowledge of the presence of the contraband and his ability to maintain control over it may be inferred." _Id._(emphasis in original). However, if the property where the contraband "is found is in _joint_ rather than exclusive possession of the accused, then knowledge of the contraband's presence and the ability to control it will not

[3] . https://scholar.google.com/

   scholar_case?case=3666561008906535914&q=ackon+v+state&hl=en&as_sdt=80006

[4] . https://scholar.google.com/

   scholar_case?case=13086129895218039019&q=ackon+v+state&hl=en&as_sdt=80006

[5] . https://scholar.google.com/

   scholar_case?case=7466842014922625828&q=ackon+v+state&hl=en&as_sdt=80006

be inferred from the accused's presence but must be established by independent proof." *Id.* (emphasis in original).

Here, there was NO direct testimony that the ammunition was even found in the house. Without this testimony, the State could not meet its burden of establishing beyond a reasonable doubt that the defendant knew the ammunition was in his presence or that he had the ability to maintain control over it. *Id.* We therefore reverse the defendant's conviction on the count alone and remand the case to the trial court to vacate the judgment and sentence on that count.

Reversed and Remanded.

6.https://scholar.google.com/ scholar_case?case=23357066738826175499&q=ackon+v+stat e&hl=en&as_sdt=80006

About the Author

Bernard Ackon is an advocate for prisoner's rights and continues to use his experience to help others to fight for their freedom and encourage to never give up.